YOUR ENNEAGRAM AND MONEY

YOUR ENNEAGRAM AND MONEY

Transforming Enneagram Edges Into Financial Freedom

KHARA CROSWAITE BRINDLE
HANNAH DEGROOT

Guide Point North Publishing
Colorado, U.S.A.

Guide Point North Publishing
An imprint of Journey Institute Press,
a division of 50 in 52 Journey, Inc.
www.journeyinstitutepress.org

Library of Congress Control Number: 2025930529
Names: Brindle, Khara Croswaite
Degroot, Hannah
Title: Your Enneagram and Money
Description: Colorado: Guide Point North Publishing, 2025

Identifiers: ISBN 978-1-964754-25-3 (hardcover)
978-1-964754-26-0 (paperback)
978-1-964754-27-7(ebook/kindle)

Subjects: BISAC: BUSINESS & ECONOMICS / Personal Finance /
Money Management |
SELF-HELP / Personal Growth / Success |
BODY, MIND & SPIRIT / Numerology

First Edition

Printed in the United States of America

1 2 3 14 22 45 58 59 64 70

This book is typeset in EB Garamond / Oswald

Cover Design by WiggleB Studios
Editing by: Jessica Medberry - InkWhale Editorial LLC

Contents

Introduction

Are you a fan of the Enneagram? We are! The Enneagram helps people understand their edges and think about ways to support growth and adaptation. This complex and dynamic personality tool has ancient roots. It describes nine unique archetypes of nine basic motivations that each of us falls into. The tool promotes compassion for the self and others, fostering curiosity and growth.

The Enneagram is not meant to solely focus on behavior or stereotyping. While the descriptions of the nine types can highlight people's strengths, the Enneagram is also meant to reveal the negative aspects, also known as the shadow side of each type. What makes it unique is that it also offers a specific and clear path for growth. The Enneagram is used in the professional world for leadership development and for creating a cohesive and understanding workplace culture. It also helps people, through self-discovery, to better relate to friends, romantic partners, and family.

Therapists like us love the Enneagram because it gives people insight into how to connect with themselves and best relate to others. When you engage with the Enneagram, it serves to clarify the relationship you have with yourself, as well as the relationships you have or want to have with others. So why not explore how the Enneagram informs money beliefs and money behaviors? Money impacts our relationship with ourselves, our relationship with others, and the emotional relationship we have with the items or objects we value, buy, and save in our lifetime!

By looking at Enneagram types and subtypes through the lenses of financial psychology and financial therapy, we aim to help you identify your Enneagram blind spots for growth, as well as unlock your advantageous edge for healing. These discoveries will allow you to create a meaningful, healthy, and fulfilling relationship with your money.

Our Audience

We wrote this book for people willing to take a deeper dive into Enneagram types and subtypes. This book is for you if you've struggled to make money. If you identify as an underearner. If you've found it difficult to hold onto or save money. If you are a helping professional suffering from noble poverty (more on this in Chapter 2). If you have avoided thinking about or talking about money. If you feel stuck, anxious, or bewildered by money. Or if you just can't seem to find a money strategy that aligns with your values. By coming into this book with self-compassion and curiosity, you are starting a journey to better understand your money story—the first and most crucial step a person can take toward having a better relationship with their money.

Who We Are

Khara has published eight books and is passionate about turning pain points into possibilities. This means she loves talking about topics other professional helpers wish to avoid, like leadership trauma, client suicide, and money challenges. As a Social Enneagram Type Three, perfectionist, financial therapist, and serial entrepreneur who specializes in working with helping professionals, of course she wanted to write a book to help colleagues unlock their money flow and full potential instead of facing chronic burnout. The Enneagram has been part of Khara's therapy practice for over thirteen years and is now part of her financial therapy practice for therapists. She hopes the skills and tools we explore together in this book will help you break free of money shame and scarcity to allow financial health and wellness into your life instead.

Hannah, a Self-Preservation Three, is a Licensed Professional Counselor, Certified Enneagram Coach, and career counselor. She loves helping people find passion, motivation, and fulfillment in their personal and professional lives, which is why the Enneagram fits so naturally into her therapy practice. She has been using the Enneagram for over a decade and has seen her clients' lives transform through their experience of this tool. Hannah loves helping people get out of their own way so they can succeed, and creating this book reflects her desire to do just that.

We both hope you can reach your personal and financial goals by playing to your strengths and becoming more aware of how to work through any blind spots you may have with money.

Finding Your Enneagram Type

Perhaps you picked up this book having heard about the Enneagram, but you've just scratched the surface in discovering how life-changing it can be. If you aren't confident you've pinpointed your Enneagram type, we encourage you to start there before reading further. A great tool is the *EnneaApp*, a free app that helps you narrow down your type with pointed quiz questions. Or you may be a traditionalist and take the Enneagram Compass assessment through The CP Enneagram Academy for $45. Whatever method you embrace, know that it's the start of an amazing journey to clarity on how you can show up best for yourself and others.

Here are some resources we recommend on your Enneagram self-discovery journey:

Books
- The *Complete Enneagram*, Beatrice Chestnut
- The *Road back to You*, Ian Morgan Cron and Suzanne Stabile
- The *Wisdom Of The Enneagram*, Don Richard Riso and Russ Hudson

Podcasts
- Enneagram 2.0 with Beatrice Chestnut and Uranio Paes
- Typology with Ian Morgan Cron
- The Art of Growth with Joel Hubbard and Jim Zartman

Enneagram Coaching

Hannah DeGroot (coauthor of this book) is a Chestnut Paes Certified Enneagram Coach. Her training has informed her contributions throughout this book. She can help you learn your dominant type and subtype through a sixty-minute typing interview. Additionally, you can engage in Enneagram coaching for deeper personal growth if desired. Contact Hannah at admin@methodandmindcoaching.com.

Introduction to Enneagram Subtypes and Centers of Intelligence

If you felt compelled to read this book, you likely already know your Enneagram type. You probably also know that there are essentially nine different motivations that drive each of us. You are born with your unique Enneagram type already in place, and it does not change over time, although your personality may present differently depending on the circumstances you experience. The nine core motivations are as follows:

1. To be good
2. To be loved
3. To be approved of
4. To be significant
5. To be competent
6. To be secure
7. To be happy
8. To be in control
9. To be peaceful

What you may not know is that each Enneagram type can be distinguished much further. Thanks to the Enneagram teachings of Beatrice Chestnut and Uranio Paes, we (the authors) believe that there are actually twenty-seven different Enneagram types. This is because each type can be broken into three subtypes: Self-Preservation, Social, and One-to-One. These subtypes come from three of the basic instincts we feel as human beings. While we all experience aspects of these instincts, one of them drives our thinking and feeling more than the other two. Learning your Enneagram subtype will bring depth to your self-understanding that the Enneagram alone cannot reveal. While this book is not meant to help you determine your subtype, you may figure it out as you read how the instincts influence your type's relationship with money. For now, we will introduce the instincts briefly below.

The **Self-Preservation instinct** seeks comfort and security, is vigilant regarding safety, and focuses on having control and structure in life. Those with this subtype often have a desire for organization and are typically more anxious, self-focused, risk-avoidant, and concerned about their health than the other subtypes. When individuals with this subtype over rely on these qualities, they may live with the feeling that their lives are constantly in danger.

The **Social instinct** has a strong focus on community alliances, and people with this subtype focus on their position and relationship to the group. They are often influential and well connected. They tend to be good communicators who are others-focused, and they direct energy toward important relationships. When these qualities are over relied upon, individuals with this subtype may exaggerate the need to be important to a group, gaining status and influence for their own protection.

The **One-to-One instinct** is often referred to as the sexual instinct; however, the term One-to-One depicts the core of the instinct well. Those with this subtype focus on close relationships. These might be intimate partnerships or close friendships, but in both cases, they have a strong desire to experience a deep connection with another being. This subtype can be marked by intensity in various areas, such as relationships, emotions, communication, risk-taking, and competition. People with this subtype may even be possessive, aggressive, and seductive to get their needs met. When these qualities are over relied upon, these individuals may see the other as the most important person in their lives, even more important than themselves.

The most important aspect of working with instincts is viewing them through the context of the unique Enneagram type. You cannot know your subtype by solely reading the short descriptions above. Just as the Enneagram types are influenced by the subtype, each of the subtypes manifests differently depending on the core type it is coupled with. In short, your dominant type + your instinct = your subtype.

The other important consideration when learning about the Enneagram is to understand the passion of each type. The **passion** is the emotional state that drives a person's thoughts, feelings, and behaviors. When it remains unconscious and unattended, a person's passion will have control of them rather than the other way around. You must consider how your type's passion interacts with the instinct. In order to grow, one must identify the ways their passion shows up in their life, and make a concerted effort to change.

In some cases, the instinct and the passion of the Enneagram type work in tandem to exaggerate the individual's feelings or behaviors. For example, a One-to-One Type Eight is the most assertive, risk-taking, and emotional of the Eights due to the intensity of the One-to-One instinct coupled with the passion of lust.

On the other hand, sometimes the instinct and the passion of the type contradict each other. These specific pairings are called **countertypes**. For instance, the One-to-One Type Six is considered a countertype because while the Type Six passion of fear drives this type to be more vigilant, skeptical, and cautious, the One-to-One instinct introduces the opposite energy. This manifests itself in a Type Six who denies their fear and takes more risks than the other two subtypes. There are nine countertypes on the Enneagram, and we will speak to these specifically in the chapters that follow. As you consider your Enneagram type and possible subtype, be aware that both the passion and the instinct are going to influence your relationship with money.

The last aspects of the Enneagram that we want you to consider are the different **Centers of Intelligence**. The Enneagram can be divided into three sections: the Body Triad (Types Eight, Nine, and One), the Heart Triad (Types Two, Three, and Four), and the Head Triad (Types Five, Six, and Seven). We refer to these as Centers of Intelligence because, based on where your type falls, certain themes will correspond across several types. Think of your Center as the primary way you navigate through and interpret the world around you. We will briefly describe each of them here.

The Body Triad is a group that uses intuition and energy to understand the world. While people of these types may have difficulty explaining some of their decisions, they can trust their gut and are usually right when they listen to it. Each type in the Body Triad is concerned with justice and fairness, and they all have a primary fear of anger, though each type will relate to this emotion differently.

The Heart Triad types primarily use emotional intelligence, feelings, and relational connections to navigate the world around them. They are concerned with image, and they need a connection with another person so that they can establish how they feel about themselves. These types experience a core emotion of shame, though again, this will manifest differently depending on the unique type.

The Head Triad types use logic, analysis, and thinking to interpret the world around them. They are each driven by the core emotion of fear, and are concerned with safety and security in varying ways. People in the Head Triad often think about feelings rather than experiencing them, and they observe others to make logical decisions about whether they can trust them. The head is the source of all the energy for these types, causing them to struggle to turn off their thoughts.

Not only do you want to consider your dominant type and subtype, but viewing your relationship with money through the lens of your Center of Intelligence will help you better understand how to use your edge to reach your money goals. It will also help you avoid money pitfalls that may be associated with the types in your triad.

Interviews and Identity Protection

As authors and licensed therapists, we took it upon ourselves to brainstorm hypotheses about each Enneagram type and their money behaviors based on our experiences serving professional helpers. Then we interviewed folks to further explore money themes related to saving, spending, and emotions. Here are the questions we asked:

1. Can you confirm your Enneagram type?
2. How would you describe your current relationship with money?
3. What emotions do you associate with money?
4. What's one of your biggest money strengths?
5. What's one of your biggest money challenges?
6. What's the best advice you've been given about money?
7. What's the worst advice you've been given about money?
8. What do you want for your future relationship with money?

We found it fascinating to note who jumped into our calendar first to talk about their current relationship with money. These were the Enneagram Ones, Twos, and Nines. Our biggest challenge was finding Enneagram Fives, Sixes, and Sevens who were willing to schedule an interview. It was fascinating to witness, and the experience reinforced some ideas we had about Enneagram types and money behaviors!

We will share stories throughout this book to further illustrate Enneagram types and money beliefs; however, many details have been omitted or changed, including names, to protect identities. Additionally, some of the people described in this book are composites of several people we've worked with professionally.

Structure of This Book

This book is organized into three parts. Part I looks at people's money challenges, focusing specially on underearners and helping professionals. We explore the money scripts, money beliefs, noble poverty, and financial trauma that values-driven helpers may experience.

In Part II, we examine each of the nine Enneagram types in light of relational and individual challenges with money, as well as motivators for meaningful shifts toward a healthier relationship with money. We refer to these bigger themes of each Enneagram type as edges, in an effort to capture the challenges that people with each type face with money, as well as reinforcing their advantages and strengths. Last, we examine subtypes and generalized behaviors with money, then illustrate them through stories that highlight, validate, and inspire meaningful change. The stories may appear overly simple and are written to capture a possible theme and result. By no means do these depictions fully reflect the true complexity or unique circumstances of each individual, nor should they be seen as a guarantee that everyone will find the same success on a similar financial path. We include them to help you connect to aspects of others' stories and be inspired by the growth paths depicted in this book.

Finally, in Part III, we introduce simple, streamlined tools to increase money flow in your personal and professional life through the lens of financial therapy. We look at strategies for saving, spending, and earning to help you take your money healing to the next level. And no, we don't subscribe to shame, scarcity, or budgeting either!

The tools featured here are for educational purposes only and do not replace a therapy session or consultation with a trained professional. However, we believe the content of this book can support you in starting your money healing journey. We are eager to share a powerful mindset shift and tools that are informed by our own work as professional helpers, therapists, and former underearners. Together, we can embrace the Enneagram to discover new ways to relate to money. Let's get started!

Chapter

Money Beliefs of Underearners

Before we explore each Enneagram type and its associated money story in detail, let's look at overarching themes for folks who struggle to make enough money. We refer to people in this group as underearners. When underearners look at their funds, they realize they aren't making enough to support the lifestyle they have or the lifestyle they want. We want to emphasize that the solution is not about cutting expenses or living in deprivation with a rigid budget of eating instant noodles every meal. Instead, it's important to recognize that folks need to make more money to live the way they want.

Maybe you can recall the price of gas when you started driving. If you continued to budget for that same price in the present, you'd be ignoring the cost of inflation and setting yourself up for failure. It's the mental shift of "I have to stop eating out/buying coffee/seeing friends to save money" to "How can I make the money I need to eat out/buy coffee/see my friends this month?" Once folks make this shift—from restriction and depriving themselves of things that they enjoy to a focus on making more—they finally feel like they can take some control back.

In the short term, this might look like selling something they own, doing a rideshare service, or picking up extra work or projects. In the long term, it might mean a steady side hustle, a second job, intentional investments or savings, raising rates in their business, or asking for a raise from their employer to get one step closer to the life they want.

Money Beliefs

As part of a money mindset shift, underearners can benefit from identifying their money beliefs. According to Rick Kahler, financial therapist and a founding member of the Financial Therapy Association, the average person has fifty to two hundred money beliefs. These ever-present beliefs about money influence our decisions and behaviors with our finances.

Here's an invitation to imagine your beliefs on a spectrum of negative to positive beliefs. Sometimes we ask clients to map these beliefs visually by writing them out or sketching them onto the spectrum just to see how they land! What are some money beliefs you hold?

Examples of Money Beliefs:
- There's never enough money.
- Money doesn't grow on trees.
- I have to work hard for my money.
- Money is unpredictable.
- Money isn't stable.
- Money is bad.
- Money is corrupt.
- It's not about the money.
- We don't talk about money.
- Money changes people.
- Money is confusing.
- Money is controlling.
- Money is limiting.
- I'm bad with money.
- I can't hold on to money.
- I can't be trusted with money.
- Money should be saved.
- Money should be spent.
- Money is a tool.
- Money is transactional.
- I'm in control of my money.
- Money is necessary.
- Money is happiness.
- Money is power.

- Money is comfort.
- Money is stability.
- Money is freedom.

As you can imagine, underearners tend to have more negative money beliefs than positive ones. These beliefs inform their behaviors regarding money and add to their struggle with earning. For example, if someone believes money is bad, they may unconsciously reject opportunities to earn more money or avoid holding on to it so they won't be seen as bad or corrupt themselves. This could look like not asking for a raise, saying yes to a job that pays them poorly, or giving their money to friends, family, and social causes rather than saving. In our work as helping professionals, it's common to hear statements like "It shouldn't be about the money. I have to be helpful. I don't want to be seen as greedy. I don't want to be a sellout." A person with these beliefs may subscribe to noble poverty, which we will talk about further in Chapter 2.

Financial Therapy Exercise #1: Word Association
Are you unsure what some of your money beliefs are? As a financial therapist, Khara loves introducing a word association to her clients. Notice what thoughts, sensations, and beliefs come to mind, and write them down for each of the words below:
- Savings
- Debt
- Credit card
- Wealth
- Rich

By getting curious about their responses to these words, people start to uncover their money beliefs.

A second aspect of identifying and healing money messages is to remain curious about what you were taught to believe about money from family, friends, society, and first bosses. What did your parents or caregivers teach you about money? What did they say? What did they do?

We've had clients who recall parents who never spoke about money. Caregivers who experienced daily calls from creditors. Families who fought about money. Siblings who stole money. Individuals who helped parents earn money from a young age. Fathers who said, "We can't afford that." Mothers who said, "Marry rich." Grandparents who declared everyone should save money at all costs. Society that says you have to hustle and grind to earn wealth. Immigrants who pass down the generational-trauma belief that they have to work hard to make money in order to make something of themselves. Various cultures that say laziness equals poverty, disgust and judgment from others. First bosses who tell employees they must "earn their stripes" and work hard for minimal wages. And the list goes on.

If you are feeling overwhelmed by the money beliefs you may hold, you are not alone. There's a lot to ponder when thinking of how they've shaped your current relationship with money. Here's a second exercise that might help.

Financial Therapy Exercise #2: First Money Memory
Close your eyes or put them at rest by looking down. Take a breath. Float back in time and recall one of your earliest memories of money. What do you notice? What feelings do you associate with that memory? What body sensations? What money belief is tied to that memory? Do you have other similar messages from other money memories? Write them down, staying curious about any connections or themes that may show up.

Money Scripts

Speaking of themes in your money beliefs, are you familiar with the concept of money scripts? Financial Psychologist Dr. Brad Klontz developed a quiz to identify a person's leanings toward one of four money scripts, which can capture some beliefs and behaviors folks have about money. However, the scripts can feel pretty pathologizing too. When we introduce the four scripts to clients, we give the disclaimer that the results capture pretty black-and-white thinking about money behaviors and aren't for everyone. With this in mind, some folks find validation in fitting one of the four scripts because it helps them normalize their experience, or they discover they aren't alone in struggling with certain money behaviors. Much like the Enneagram, it helps them discover their growth edges and warning signs for when things feel off balance. Therefore, we included the four scripts as part of the self-discovery journey for underearners as well.

1. Money Avoidant
Core Belief: Let's not think or talk about money.
Essence: anxiety, dread, discomfort, negative body response
Behaviors: Avoidance in the form of
- not checking accounts
- not tracking spending
- experiencing somatic distress when thinking about money
- failing a budget
- not advocating for increased income

Consequences: The head-in-the-sand mentality can prevent a person from making progress on their money goals. It can also prevent them from asking for help until things feel dire, such as being in collections, considering bankruptcy, or receiving a letter from the IRS.

Sammy
Sammy is a passionate therapist who works for an agency serving kids and families. Almost three years into the field, she gets a job offer that would allow her to work more hours and earn more money. Sammy is struggling to determine how much money she needs for her expenses every month. She has avoided checking her bank account because it causes feelings of stress and shame, and as a result, she continues to come up short on funds at the end of each month to pay her bills. Instead of looking at her numbers, Sammy has learned to rely on her parents to lend her money until she can pay them back.

2. Money Focus
Core Belief: More money would make me happier.
Essence: fixation, money control, pursuit
Behaviors:
- Chasing milestones
- Goalposts moving to reflect more and more money wanted/ needed
- Panic when asked, "What is enough?"

- Can embody generosity in celebrating and spending money on others they care about

Consequences: This script can cause a person to struggle with saving money. It encourages financial dependence on others, limits success in meeting money goals because goalposts continue to change, and incurs a higher risk of workaholism.

Tran

Tran comes from a hardworking immigrant family that taught her to save as much as she could from a very young age. Although she has achieved her original goal of $1 million saved for retirement, all she feels is anxiety. Tran is recognizing that her goalpost has already moved to $2 million in her head, making it hard to celebrate the milestone of saving $1 million in her career so far. Because her anxiety about money remains high regardless of how much she has saved, Tran is burned out in a job that takes a lot of her energy away from her family.

3. Money Status

Core Belief: I've worked hard for my money, I'm going to show it.

Essence: self esteem, sense of belonging, and self-worth is net worth

Behaviors:

- May gravitate toward labels and name brands so others will observe their wealth
- Subscribes to the "keeping up with the Joneses" mentality
- Invests in nice houses, cars, tech, and toys as signs of success

Note: This script is more common in young adults who are earning good money for the first time in their adult lives.

Consequences: People who ascribe to this script have difficulty saving money, experience the dopamine chase of buying, and confuse signs of wealth with signs of respect.

Candy

Candy comes from humble beginnings. She was raised in a trailer park with her two siblings in a small Midwestern town. When she receives her first paycheck after college, she is making more money than she's ever experienced. Candy is exhilarated, feeling like she finally has the funds to dress the way she wants others to see her, with a wardrobe very different from the hand-me-down clothes and shoes of her upbringing. Her first purchase with her new paycheck is a designer coat which she recognizes she can't truly afford. She tells herself she will put it on her credit card and pay it off with her next paycheck when it comes due.

4. Money Vigilant

Core Belief: Don't spend money, save it!

Essence: weather the storm, be prepared, scarcity

Behaviors:

- Strong desire to save money
- Celebrates being thrifty or is a maximizer researching to get the best deal
- May go out of their way to get a deal, like driving forty minutes across town for the cheapest gas, or keeping several shopping tabs open on their browser to track when an item goes on sale

Consequences: People with this script experience a scarcity mindset. They are great at saving (with the risk of hoarding money), have limited quality of life experiences, and experience immediate distress or guilt after making any large purchase, including necessary ones.

Natalie

Natalie recognizes she is spending way too much time researching and attempting to find the best deals for her purchases. The mental energy this involves is causing her to fall behind at work and disrupting her sleep several times a week. Her attempts to maximize her saving potential are keeping her anxiety elevated until she finds the perfect deal to finally click "buy now." Admittedly, this process feels like the only way she can reduce the shame and guilt that show up with bigger purchases. She wants to gamify her system of completing purchases to make it more tolerable. Meanwhile, she is losing hours each week to the mental labor of determining how to best save money.

As you can see, each of the four money scripts provides a negative lens with which to examine money behaviors. Considering our parents or caregivers with this awareness of money scripts can be a powerful exercise. Did their money beliefs influence us? Absolutely!

Are some of those money beliefs still with us? Yes! Gaining clarity regarding their modeling and the source of some money beliefs can start the healing process for underearners.

Of the four scripts, folks often find the Money Focus and Money Vigilant scripts more tolerable, but even these scripts can manifest as unhealthy and extreme at times. Let's take a closer look at scarcity and noble poverty—the outcomes of negative money beliefs and extreme money behaviors for underearners—in the next chapter.

Chapter 2

Signs of Noble Poverty and Scarcity

We mentioned noble poverty in the previous chapter as the natural outcome for underearners with unhealed negative beliefs about money. Noble poverty is the experience of sacrificing our own financial well-being for the benefit of others. It has a flavor of martyrdom, featuring thoughts like "I did this for them. I did it because I'm a good person. I'm a helper, after all."

But forgoing money for the sake of helping others is a dangerous way to approach personal finance, and it serves as a major contributor to professional burnout. Noble poverty affects helping professionals, including therapists, social workers, nurses, and nonprofit leaders. Here are some factors that may make someone susceptible to noble poverty:

- People-pleasing tendencies
- Being female
- Enneagram Type Two or Nine
- Perfectionism
- Working in helping professions
- Working for a business with a nonprofit structure
- A mission to serve the underserved
- Negative money beliefs
- Family or social beliefs that money is corrupt, evil, or bad
- Being raised on Disney movies

Did we surprise you with that last one? Think about it. Who has the money in Disney movies? The evil kings and queens. The villains. If you were raised on Disney movies, you were subjected to messages about money being evil, bad, or corrupt from a very young age—which absolutely contributes to your beliefs about money.

Again, beliefs shape behaviors. How do you know you are experiencing noble poverty? Similar to money avoidance, you might:

- Avoid thinking or talking about money.
- Resist asking for a raise or negotiating a salary.
- Accept a low-paying job for a cause.
- Struggle with financial hardships because of helping others.
- Donate money you don't have.
- Focus on generosity over saving for your own financial goals.
- Believe that financial hardship is normal.
- Not advocate for yourself, because you don't want to be accused of selling out or being greedy.

Suffering from Scarcity

Another aspect of an underearner's money story is scarcity. By definition, scarcity sounds like "There isn't enough." Not enough clients, not enough money. Living in scarcity contributes to poor boundaries and workaholism, and these factors increase risks of resentment, health conditions, and burnout for helping professionals. Let's explore seven signs of scarcity that many therapists and coaches experience when self-employed, recognizing their application to other self-employed helping professions as well.

#1 You say yes to a client who's not a good fit.

Taking on any and every client that calls can be a sign of scarcity. As professional helpers, we aren't a good fit for everyone, so we should use caution and practice pausing before taking on clients that aren't within our wheelhouse. It can also become an ethical concern if we take on a client who would benefit from a specialty that we aren't trained in.

Scarcity Solution: Identify your ideal client(s) and market to them!

#2 You schedule a client on your lunch break to make their schedule work.

We've been guilty of this too. The client shares that they have a limited schedule, so you offer them your lunch hour to make it work.

This could become a recipe for burnout if you're not taking the much-needed break to rest, eat, and reset during a day full of clients.

Scarcity Solution: Block out your lunches and honor them.

#3 You schedule a client at a time that's not ideal for your schedule.

Your client shares that their schedule is changing and their original appointment time won't work any longer. So you respond by suggesting a Friday or later evening appointment that you don't actually offer to other clients on your caseload. This response of "fitting people in" could lead to burnout or resentment if clients expect scheduling exceptions regularly, especially since you set your schedule to honor important things in your life, such as family, self-care, or other obligations.

Scarcity Solution: Commit to a work schedule to see how you like it. When you identify that schedule, honor it with new and existing clients. You can always change the schedule later as you see fit—it's a benefit of working for yourself!

#4 You feel uncomfortable with a blank spot in your calendar, so you seek to fill it.

Perhaps you find yourself nervous with too many open appointment slots in your calendar, so you attempt to track down clients who haven't scheduled in a while or seek projects to keep yourself feeling busy.

Scarcity Solution: Lean into the discomfort. Schedule self-care or a fun project in the free space. Embrace boredom as the catalyst for creativity.

#5 When you have a lighter schedule, you take on more clients than you actually need to.

Your efforts to take on new clients or add in new commitments leaves you feeling stretched too thin the following week or month when folks are scheduling regularly again.

Scarcity Solution: Identify a mantra or phrase you can say to yourself when things feel too light and anxiety-provoking. Choose something that helps you hold fast against an urge to take on more or be overly busy. Examples: "Productivity over busyness"; "Discomfort can lead to growth."

#6 You hesitate to raise your rates or move to private pay from insurance because you're afraid you'll lose clients.
As a helping professional, it is possible that you could lose a handful of clients when shifting away from insurance or raising your rates. Preparing for that possibility can help you feel in control of next steps in response. However, it's important to recognize that avoiding a change that would benefit you, your practice, or your family from a business or burnout standpoint is a textbook example of scarcity when working for yourself.

Scarcity Solution: Gently remind yourself that folks don't like to start over with new providers if they can make things work financially. Revisit your numbers to clarify why a pivot to private pay or a higher rate is worthwhile to you in your practice. Then make a conscious plan for the transition that supports both you and your clients through the change.

#7 You see colleagues as competition rather than collaboration.
You notice a colleague is doing something similar to you, such as serving the same client population or offering a course or training with similar content. Feeling threatened and responding as if they are competition is a sign of scarcity. Instead, recognize that you each have your own style, and cross-referring could be helpful for reaching more folks who want particular services or content. This mindset shift could result in a beautiful collaboration where you both win!

Scarcity Solution: Recognize that you have your own spin on things and that there are plenty of people looking for what you offer. Network with that colleague to get to know them better. This response reduces the internal narrative that they are a competitor. Instead, choose to see them as a fellow professional and potential referral source.

Avoiding scarcity thinking means shifting our mindset and healing those negative beliefs that shape our money story. Healing also requires remaining curious about more subtle signs of scarcity. Consider crafting your personalized list of warning signs using the journal prompts in Appendix B. This exercise is yet another way to empower you to transform your future self in your relationship with money.

Next, let's explore financial trauma as it relates to the formation of noble poverty and scarcity behaviors.

Chapter

Understanding Financial Trauma

Another aspect of healing your relationship with money is rec-ognizing financial trauma and how it has contributed to the narrative that is your money story.

Our Enneagram type is defined at birth, and it doesn't change because of trauma. What does fluctuate, however, is how our patterns of behavior change under stressful situations in contrast to healthy circumstances. Stress behaviors have the potential to unlock awareness about our shadow selves, which we lovingly refer to as Enneagram edges throughout this book. From this point of view, our stress responses spotlight opportunities for meaningful growth and change. Additionally, how we show up in good health or wellness is important to recognize in our self-awareness journey, in order to support our individualized trauma work.

Financial trauma is one trauma we can work toward healing. It is defined by each person and is considered impactful and disruptive, like so many other traumas folks can experience. Our colleague Nathan Astle, a Certified Financial Therapist, describes financial trauma as a combination of stressors that contribute to major (big) or frequent (small and repeated) body withdrawals. These leave us depleted, bringing on fight/flight/freeze responses. Nathan describes how being "in the red" in this body bank account has all sorts of consequences that may lead the person suffering to seek professional help to heal.

Ultimately, each person gets to say what is and is not financial trauma for them based on how the experience has impacted them physically, emotionally, relationally, and financially. In other words, professionals don't define financial trauma, their clients do. Keeping this in mind, here are some examples of financial trauma for ongoing reflection.

Examples of Financial Trauma:
- Loan discrimination
- Housing discrimination
- The Great Depression
- Eviction and/or homelessness
- Family fighting about money
- Domestic violence and financial control
- Inheritance
- Recession
- Job loss
- Medical crisis
- Divorce
- Death of spouse
- Family loss
- Generational debt
- Financial infidelity
- Financial abuse
- Credit card fraud
- Gambling loss
- Identity theft

How would any of these experiences impact you? In Chapter 18, we will list some other financial stressors, and your responses to these might be very different. As with other traumas, having access to supportive communities and resources can reduce the long-term impact of financial trauma, allowing a person to regain their physical and emotional footing. Let's look at a few favorite tools that can support the healing process.

Possible Tools for Healing
- Emotional Freedom Technique (EFT)
- Core Beliefs Exercise
- Dear Money Letter

Emotional Freedom Technique (EFT)

The Emotional Freedom Technique is a tapping tool meant to regulate the nervous system by stimulating various pressure points. What makes it approachable for financial trauma is that it's a tool for the present, and there is no need to reframe negative thoughts or emotions while engaging in the practice. Instead, a person names the thoughts and feelings they have in the moment as they tap the points in a pattern, while noticing any shifts within their body.

For example, an individual may voice something like, "I can't believe I'm stuck in credit card debt again. I'm so embarrassed. My stomach is in knots. Why do I keep doing this to myself?" As they hear their thoughts and feelings out loud, in tandem with the tapping, the emotional charge is often reduced. They may naturally move into cognitive reframes, such as "Shaming myself doesn't make change happen. This can get better. I can ask for help to make a change with my finances." Here's how tapping looks:

Step 1: Review the list of EFT tapping points.
- The heel of your hand
- Your inner eyebrow
- Your temple
- The place where your under eye meets your cheekbone
- The skin between your nose and your lip
- The skin between your chin and your lip
- Your collarbone
- Your lowest rib at your side
- The top of your head

Step 2: Identify any negative or charged sensations in your body as you recall your money worries or stressors. Begin by tapping the heel of your hand with your opposite hand. Name out loud your worries or stressors connected to money, without censoring, reframing, or revising your word choice.

Step 3: Move down the list of tapping points as you express your emotions out loud. Allow your worries or thoughts to come to you as you tap.

Step 4: Complete three or more cycles of tapping as you move down the tapping points on your body. Notice any shifts in the negative sensations that were present at the beginning of the exercise. Notice which tapping spots you found most comforting or liked best. Repeat your tapping cycle as needed for the desired positive shift in sensations and emotions.

EFT is a great tool for addressing emotions, stressors, and trauma triggers that are happening in the present. Next, let's look at an exercise that focuses on the past as well.

Core Beliefs Exercise

Getting to the root of our behaviors is another valuable trauma technique because it brings things into the light that we can then begin to heal or change. The Core Beliefs Exercise allows us to look at the past and the present.

It isn't something to dive into without proper time and space, however. Why? It feels intense and vulnerable to sit in beliefs that we tend to suppress deep down inside. Such beliefs are often hidden and rooted at the core of who we are. It's necessary to give the disclaimer that this exercise is powerful and emotionally charged. Naming your core belief when you have a visceral response to it feels like being kicked in the gut; you may experience waves of nausea or a desire to cry. Traumas of all kinds can reinforce these beliefs. Here's how the exercise works:

Step 1: Grab a piece of paper or a journal. Self-worth is deeply rooted in beliefs we carry based on our earliest experiences in life. To make these core beliefs more approachable for self-discovery, let's use a visual. Draw a picture of a tree with leaves, trunk, and roots, or grab our Your Enneagram and Money Workbook for a tree template.

Step 2: The worries and anxieties we are consciously aware of are the leaves of the tree. These are the things we can easily verbalize, such as stressors and concerns. Things like "I'm always broke. I feel like a bad partner when I can't stick to our budget. I'm always running behind on bills. I don't speak up for what I want financially." What are your worries and anxieties related to money? Write them in the leaves of the tree.

Step 3: Going deeper cognitively, ask yourself what these thoughts say about you. You may recognize thoughts like, "I'm stupid with money. I can't be trusted with money. I need someone else to manage my money." Write down key phrases or thoughts on the trunk of your tree.

Step 4: Continue to ask yourself the question, "If this is true about me, what does this say about me?" This will help you go even deeper and get to the roots of the tree. The roots represent the negative core beliefs that drive behaviors and can feel painful to explore. Negative core beliefs sound like, "I am unlovable. I'm a failure. I'm unworthy." Capture your negative core beliefs in the roots of your tree.

Step 5: Now that you are aware of your negative core beliefs, what would you prefer to believe? Write the opposite of your negative core beliefs or another, more positive belief to the side of your tree. Make sure it's an "I" statement! Try on statements like, "I am lovable as I am. I'm trying the best I can. I am worthy." Which new beliefs are easier to embrace or accept?

How can knowing your core belief inform your money healing journey? It's another way to uncover money beliefs that dictate your behaviors! What are your warning signs that your negative core beliefs are driving your financial behaviors? Signs of scarcity? Signs of noble poverty? Signs of avoidance? Make note of these warning signs as part of this exercise for additional reflection.

The last exercise integrates the past, present, and future for financial trauma healing. Where are you headed? How will you know when you are feeling healthy and healed? What signs will you look for as proof of your progress? Completing this last exercise several times can help you see measurable change and evolution in your money story over time.

Dear Money Letter

This exercise is inspired by Jen Sincero's book *You are a Badass at Making Money*. We love the emotional punch that a handwritten letter to money can bring to financial trauma healing. There are several variations of how this exercise can look, captured below:

Option 1: Write a letter to money, breaking up with it and removing its power from your life.
By composing a letter to money as if it were an abusive partner and you want to end the relationship, you can feel empowered to

cultivate a new relationship with money—one rooted in self-trust, empowerment, and healthier dynamics with finances. Here's one example from a client we will call Ruby:

Dear Money,

I've come to the realization that this isn't working anymore. The power you've held over me is hurting my mental health and I need a change. I'm tired of feeling shame every time I see my credit card statements. The embarrassment I feel when I can't pay the bills on time is excruciating. I don't like feeling stupid and I will no longer allow you to treat me as if I'm less than. I'm ready to have a better relationship with money, and you are not it. It's over.

Sincerely, Ruby

Option 2: Write an authentic, emotional letter to money, then have money write a letter of response to you.
What do you want to say to money? What themes would money embody in their response to you? What compassion or protection could they convey in a healed, healthy relationship with you?

Dear Money,

I've come to the realization that this isn't working anymore. The power you've held over me is making me lose a sense of who I am and I need a change. I'm tired of feeling shame every time I see my credit card statements. I'm tired of feeling embarrassed when I can't pay the bills on time. You said you'd take care of me. You promised that in having you, I'd be secure. How can I trust you when it feels like you make things harder, not easier? I know I can be better and deserve better in this relationship. I want to do this together, but I'm not sure how.

Sincerely, Ruby

Dear Ruby,

I hear what you are saying and I realize I've gone about this all wrong. I've made you feel shame and embarrassment, hoping it would prevent you from spending. I've attempted to protect you from debt, but recognize now how that has backfired. I promised security and haven't delivered on that promise. My contributions in your life have made you question yourself and your abilities, and I'm sorry. You've shared how you struggle to trust me, and I know I can do this differently. I

hope you'll give me a chance to show you that our relationship can be better, one built on trust and open communication. I really want to try.
Yours, Money

Writing these letters by hand is key. The brain–body connection and the emotions expressed through handwritten letters exceed those arising from typed ones. This is one of the many reasons therapists often make this request of clients who are willing to engage in journaling or letter-writing exercises.

First drafts are meant to be uncensored, and may be full of hurt, anger, and other emotions that need to come out. Over time, the tone of additional letters can naturally change. Sometimes even the handwriting changes from the first cathartic draft, transforming into something more grounded and controlled in subsequent versions! Another meaningful part of this exercise? Revisiting old letters can serve as encouragement and evidence of how far a person has come on their money healing journey.

Financial Trauma Healing Modalities

In addition to the exercises introduced above, various therapeutic approaches can be applied to the healing of financial trauma. Although this is not an exhaustive list, we want to highlight some modalities that are being introduced into financial therapy spaces. These techniques are showing promising results for clients who want to reduce money shame, address financial trauma, and decrease financial anxiety, to name a few possible benefits.

- Cognitive Behavioral Therapy (CBT)
- Emotionally Focused Couples Therapy (EFCT)/Attachment-Focused Financial Therapy
- Internal Family Systems (IFS)
- Narrative Therapy
- Solution-Focused Therapy (SFT)

Cognitive Behavioral Therapy (CBT)

Theoretical Assumptions: Thoughts impact feelings and behaviors. Negative beliefs can contribute to unwanted behaviors and distress. Positive beliefs support healthy behavioral change.

Goal(s) of CBT Financial Therapy: Reduce negative thought patterns and reinforce positive thought patterns for behavior change with money. Increase clients' successful problem solving in response to financial stressors and help them improve their money practices.

Emotionally Focused Couples Therapy (EFCT)/Attachment-Focused Financial Therapy

Theoretical Assumptions: Relationships can improve through de-escalation, identifying patterns to conflict, restructuring interactions, and defining new interaction patterns.

Goal(s) of Attachment-Focused Couples Financial Therapy: Create a stronger emotional connection in relationships. Understand the Couples Conflict Cycle. Recognize emotions that drive behaviors in order to support conflict resolution involving financial stressors. Identify values-based spending and saving. Improve communication skills for long-lasting relationships.

Internal Family Systems (IFS)

Theoretical Assumptions: Developing Self-led leadership fosters inner harmony, unburdens parts of Self for healthy functioning, and supports cohesion for authentic living.

Goal(s) of IFS Financial Therapy: Identify parts driving money behaviors, unburden those parts, and approach money decisions from Self for grounded, purposeful money management, including Self-led spending and saving.

Narrative Therapy

Theoretical Assumptions: Clients can learn to use the power of story to identify problems in progress and rewrite or broaden those stories. Through this process, they make room for positive stories and thoughts about themselves.

Goal(s) of Narrative Financial Therapy: Externalize money problems from the person. Break down problematic narratives and rewrite empowered narratives about the self and one's finances. Explore societal influence on personal narrative of money while working to write a new story about money.

Solution-Focused Therapy (SFT)

Theoretical Assumptions: People are motivated to change. Therapists can utilize a person's strengths to support change. Change happens in the present. Small steps support change. The client is the expert in their own life.

Goal(s) of Solution-Focused Financial Therapy: Collaborate to support measurable changes with money. If a money strategy isn't working, trying something different supports change.

Empowering folks to find a professional is one step towards treating financial trauma. It is important to ask about the provider's approach, training, and experience to improve the chances of a good fit for the supportive work that is person-centered financial trauma healing. In the next chapter, we will introduce some healthy money scripts that helpers and underearners have embraced in their quest for money healing.

Chapter 4

Healing Money Scripts

When we introduced Dr. Brad Klontz's money scripts in Chapter 1, we acknowledged they can feel pathologizing and negative unless viewed through the Enneagram lens of pinpointing edges for growth. Now we'd like to look at your edges on a healthy continuum, where your Enneagram type can inform your psychological advantage. It can also help you determine strategies that are optimal for you in your relationship with your finances. Here are three healing money scripts that clients have embodied on their journey to a healthier relationship with money.

- Money Optimism
- Money Harmony
- Money Plentiful

Money Optimism

Core Belief: When it comes to money, it will all work out.

Essence: hope, hands-off approach, intuition, passive energy, gut feeling

Behaviors:

- Resourceful due to a belief that things will work out in the end.

36

- The client may be more open to taking risks with their money, such as investing, diversifying income streams, or spending on bigger purchases without the angst of attempting to get the best deal.

Consequences: Greater possibility of financial growth. Willingness to take more risks. Potential struggle with managing money if chasing several leads at once (think Enneagram Sevens).

Types Compatible with Money Optimism Script:

- Enneagram Fours: helps redirect envy into authenticity in their desire to do things their way.
- Enneagram Sevens: supports their love of more, including spontaneity and abundance, coupled with the desire for flexibility.

Sonya

Sonya describes herself as optimistic with money. She lacks anxiety and has steady self-assurance. Over the years, she has invested in several businesses to add to her income streams and grow wealth. She holds a lot of hope for the future and needs to do some work around knowing her numbers to meet her goals more efficiently. Sonya learns how to manage her "bright, shiny object" parts as an entrepreneur and how to "plug the leaks" on out-of-sight expenses. These strategies help her take home the most money possible, getting her closer to her long-term money goals.

Lorelle

Lorelle has an opportunity to buy a private practice she feels could build her wealth as a business owner. She finds herself daydreaming about the lifestyle changes she could embrace, like finally buying her dream car. But three months after the business is hers, Lorelle feels like she is drowning in unanticipated expenses. Instead of taking home more money, she feels like she's adding to her debt. Lorelle seeks a business consultant to help her ensure that the practice is running as it should. She finds reassurance in her consultant and several books that emphasize the typical business growth patterns: years of learning, earning, and then scaling. With this knowledge and regular meetings with her financial adviser, Lorelle finds herself back in a place of optimism instead of overwhelm regarding her earning potential.

Money Harmony

Core Belief: Money comes and money goes; money flows.

Essence: hands on, active energy, anxiety reduction, manifesting, self-trust, energy, flow

Behaviors:

- Embraces the flow and movement of money; does not seek stagnation in spending and saving.
- Holds confidence that money will come in when needed.

Consequences: Reduced anxiety about money. Money feels more neutral, more transactional.

Types Compatible with Money Harmony Script:

- Enneagram Ones: aids in their quest to reduce anger and the resulting rigidity in their thinking, creating more balance.
- Enneagram Twos: helpful when taking pride in their helpfulness to others while also tending to their own financial needs.
- Enneagram Sixes: undertaken out of fear and loyalty toward others while seeking security and stability in their financial lives.
- Enneagram Nines: beneficial when seeking to rediscover their own needs in tandem with the needs of others.

Kiersten

Kiersten worked hard to heal her own "money stuff" before starting a business of her own. Although she experiences stress at times about her fluctuating practice numbers, she maintains a money flow mindset. This includes maintaining quality relationships with referral sources and experimenting with other income streams. Kiersten recently launched a secondary income stream in addition to her client work, which has opened doors to new opportunities for networking and collaboration within her community.

Ester

Ester is a big believer in the energy things have, including money. She's lived her adult life witnessing that things come full circle. This perspective allows her to spend money with ease, knowing she's created spaciousness and systems for money to come back into her life. Recently, Ester's car required new tires, which felt like a big expense. In a matter of days, she was also approached to give a paid presentation on a topic she's passionate about. In Ester's mind, the presentation funds came forward energetically to help her pay for her car tires. This viewpoint feels satisfying and grounding for her in how she continues to approach her finances.

Money Plentiful

Core Belief: There is enough money.
    Essence: grounding, regulating, self-confidence, knowledge
    Behaviors:
- Confidence in manifesting and earning money.
- Uses money as a tool.

Consequences: Takes risks and embraces entrepreneurial spirit. Remains open-minded to money strategies. Ever evolving with their money.
    Types Compatible with Money Plentiful Script:
- Enneagram Threes: helpful for reducing their workaholic drive and helping them feel fulfillment in all they've accomplished.
- Enneagram Fives: aids those who seek reassurance that they are educated and therefore financially secure due to the knowledge they've gained.
- Enneagram Eights: supports a wish to reduce the amount of control they exert over their finances, believing their needs for stability and security are being met.

Amaya
Amaya recognizes her privilege in not having to stress about money. She started saving money from a young age, and now has quite the nest egg. Although Amaya is mostly happy with her numbers, she's in a place where she'd like to experiment with other wealth-building strategies so her money can work for her. She is at a stage of life where she'd like to work less and still grow her money for retirement. Therefore, Amaya makes a plan to talk with her financial professional to diversify her portfolio, wanting to explore putting a chunk of her money into a High-Yield Savings Account as another wealth strategy.

Monica

Monica went through a messy divorce before finding her way with money. She devoured dozens of courses and books over the years to improve her financial literacy, and has been a financial coach for single women for almost a decade. When talking to a friend over coffee about her business, Monica realizes she's finally "arrived" with her money: She feels confident in her ability to make it for herself and to help others earn more too. As a result, she's looking forward to launching a book on the topic of financially empowering other women within the next year.

Warning Signs with Money

Even as we explore healthier money scripts that are worth moving toward in our money healing, it's important to recognize that both healthy and unhealthy scripts live on a continuum with one another. With this in mind, it's natural for the pendulum to swing back to negative scripts, resulting in older money behaviors in times of financial stress, uncertainty, and skepticism, or in an absence of self-trust.

For example, during the COVID-19 pandemic, business owners were invited to apply for the Paycheck Protection Program (PPP), a federal relief program meant to provide funds to help businesses retain employees. As details of the PPP were presented, it felt too good to be true to some business owners. They had a hard time believing they wouldn't owe the money back, or have some other strings attached to what felt like "free money." Because of this skepticism, some business owners declined to apply or delayed their application, and lost out on money that could have helped them stay afloat before the PPP funds ran out.

What are some signs that you are backsliding into old money beliefs and money scripts? Revisit the Core Beliefs Exercise of Chapter 3 and get ready to craft a list of your unique warning signs. Consider your responses to the following questions to help you identify your warning signs.

1. What's it look like when I'm doing well with money?
- Physically
- Emotionally
- Relationally

2. What's it look like when I'm not doing well with money?
- Physically
- Emotionally
- Relationally
3. What are my triggers for backsliding into negative money scripts?
4. What can I do for myself when I'm struggling with my money behaviors?
5. What do I need from others?

Here are some examples of warning signs we've seen with clients we've served:
- Procrastination on deadlines
- Avoidance of money tasks that feel time consuming
- Delaying action out of a desire to avoid feelings of finality (i.e., It will be real if I do _____)
- Inaction and stuckness
- Fixation on saving money
- Deprivation
- Increased anxiety about budgeting and "staying the course"
- Hyperfocus on spending, including rumination, conflict, and maximizing purchases to get the best deal
- Distraction sought in other mind-numbing tasks
- Tackling other projects that feel "easier"
- Emotional or impulse spending
- Feeling stupid or incompetent with money
- Experiencing envy or judgment of others with money
- Resurfacing shame
- Negative self-talk

Dominique

Dominique identifies as having a negative money script of money focus and would like to move toward a healthier script of money harmony. She's a mental health professional who has been actively healing her money story in financial therapy when she is suddenly laid off from a startup that provides online therapy. Dominique had already realized that the company wasn't compensating her fairly, and she was in the process of finding a new job when she received the news of losing her current position. During her ongoing job search, Dominique found herself in old money habits in response to financial stress. When asked to craft her list of warning signs, here's what she shared with her financial therapist:

1. What's it look like when I'm doing well with money?
   - Physically: animated, sleeping well, no muscle aches, energy
   - Emotionally: hopeful, cheerful, grounded
   - Relationally: social, open, trusting

2. What's it look like when I'm not doing well with money?
   - Physically: lethargic, slouched posture, muscle pain, poor sleep
   - Emotionally: hopeless, irritable, anxious
   - Relationally: isolated, annoyed, experiencing conflict

3. What are my triggers for backsliding into negative money scripts?
   - Seeing my checking account amount going down
   - Having to access my savings to get by
   - Losing my job
   - Making big purchases on limited income
   - Feeling pressure to eat out with friends

4. What can I do for myself when I'm struggling with my money behaviors?
   - Review my numbers to see what I can afford this month
   - Keep applying for jobs
   - Set a budget and boundaries for eating out
   - Move my body to reduce anxiety
   - Tell myself this is temporary
   - Continue financial therapy

5. What do I need from others?
   - Compassion
   - Understanding
   - Reassurance that things are going to be okay
   - Offers to pay for food once in a while until I get back on my feet

By completing this exercise, Dominique gained a better sense of why she's backsliding into some money focus behaviors, helping her speak to herself with more compassion during this financially trying time. Additionally, she now has some ideas about what she can do for herself to regulate, as well as what she can ask from others so they can best support her.

Anchoring In with Attachment Styles and Money

Support from others is another access point for healthier money scripts in our healing journey. From the lens of attachment, our partner's money beliefs and money scripts can influence our own, just as our parents' or caregivers' money beliefs did growing up. So what would it be like to have a partner embody one of these healthier money scripts? Could it influence our own healing journey, similar to how a securely attached partner can heal some of our attachment trauma? Let's explore attachment styles briefly to see what we mean:

- Secure attachment
- Anxious attachment
- Avoidant attachment

Secure attachment is the ideal attachment type, embodying reassurance, safety, and connection.

Anxious attachment describes a dynamic of insecurity and self-doubt. A person with this attachment style may question the validity of the relationship, their self-worth, and their worthiness to the point of acting out from intense anxiety.

Avoidant attachment describes a disconnected style where a person may operate as if they don't want or need anyone or anything, responding to vulnerability and intimacy with avoidance.

In his 2012 book *Wired for Love*, Stan Tatkin describes the three attachment styles with a nautical theme for easy recall. He characterizes secure attachment as an anchor, anxious attachment as an ocean wave, and avoidant attachment as an island. Do these attachment styles and supportive imagery feel familiar? In our opinion, a person's attachment style can describe their current relationship with money, as well as their relationship with others and money.

Attachment Reflection Questions:
1. Which attachment style do you have with money? How do you know?
2. Which attachment style do you have with a partner or spouse? How do you know?
3. What attachment style would you like to have with money? Why?
4. If money could talk, what would you want it to say to you when you need reassurance?
5. What can a partner or spouse say (or do for you) that is comforting and helps you emotionally regulate?
6. What can you do for yourself when your attachment style is driving your behaviors?

Our Relationship with Money

What steps can be taken to experience a secure attachment with money? This entire book serves to get you closer to your goal of embracing that healthier relationship. In particular, Chapter 18 will present an overview of financial therapy and money skills. Can a healthy money script of Money Optimism, Money Harmony, or Money Plentiful be a measure of our success in creating a meaningful relationship with money? We'd like to think so. We will further explore this topic when we describe money meetings in Chapter 13. Money meetings can help you gain momentum with your finances, while also serving as a tool for reflection and a measure of relationship progress with money.

Money as a Partner

Imagine an infinity symbol (number eight on its side). On the right side is you: your thoughts, your feelings, your behaviors. On the left side is money: how it thinks, feels, and behaves as if it were a partner in your story. Imagine a line separating your half of the infinity symbol and money's side. This line represents an incident that sets conflict in motion between you and money. We've just described the Couples Conflict Cycle of Emotionally Focused Couples Therapy (EFCT) found in Chapter 3. The incident could be something like an unpaid bill, a medical crisis, exceeding a budget, or paying a credit card. Money can be the hero, the villain, or the enabler in your relationship.

1. When you think about the incident, what **thoughts** come up for you?
2. When you think about the thoughts, what **feelings** come with them?
3. When you think about the feelings, what **behaviors** are the result?
4. How does money respond to your behaviors? Does it help or hurt?
5. If money is adding to the conflict, what response or attachment style could money demonstrate to make things better?
6. How can your thoughts, feelings, and behaviors change for the better?

Our Relationship with Others and Money

Would it surprise you to know that, according to a 2019 study from the American Psychological Association, money remains a top stressor for Americans? Money is also a frequent point of conflict for partners and couples. How can a partner's healthy money script anchor us, allowing us to better weather a financial storm? It starts with a healthy connection with your partner or spouse when it comes to money, usually through frequent, emotionally regulated conversations about spending and saving.

Other Tools for Learning to Talk About Money:
• Healthy Wealthy Talks Conversation Deck by The Pledgettes (pledgettes.com)
• Let's Talk Finances: Couples Edition Card Deck by Your Financial Therapist on Amazon

Questions for Connection:
1. What triggers a conflict or fight with your partner/spouse about money?
2. What feelings come up for you in the conflict?
3. What does your inner critic say about you/your abilities during the conflict?
4. Where do you feel that criticism in your body?
5. What does the fight say about your relationship?

6. What reassurance do you need from your partner during the conflict to help you regulate?
7. How can you voice that need for reassurance to help you feel heard?

We know that talking about money is difficult for many people. Consider mapping your conflicts about money on the EFCT infinity symbol from the previous Money as a Partner exercise. Sometimes people can more clearly understand their partner's thoughts, feelings, and behaviors (as well as money's role in the conflict) when they see the pattern(s) mapped out this way.

Several colleagues in financial therapy say, "It isn't about the money"—it's much deeper and more emotional than that. In his work as a financial therapist for couples and people experiencing financial trauma, Nathan Astle emphasizes that the work is actually about enhancing connection, building trust, and identifying shared financial goals that can bring a couple closer together. That's when meaningful shifts with money can happen—when you work on healing attachment trauma and developing healthy money scripts for a better you.

It's important to emphasize that embodying healthy money scripts isn't a one-and-done process. It takes intentional money healing, as well as a conscious effort to avoid backsliding into the old money habits and negative money scripts that have been ingrained in us for decades. We've already identified where you can land with money beliefs and money scripts, as well as the direction in which you may want to move for growth. Now, we can explore how your Enneagram type contributes to your money story, beliefs, and behaviors for a healthier relationship with your money.

Chapter

Enneagram Ones and Money

Enneagram Type One is sometimes referred to as The Perfectionist. Type Ones are motivated by a need to be good and right. They hold an internal belief that they are good and okay if they always do the right thing, which comes from an internal compass rather than from outside rules and morals. Therefore, it's not unexpected that someone of this type may show up as a hard worker who is detail oriented, methodical, rigid, and resentful of deviations from plans. They may say things like, "We've always done it this way. That's not correct. It's working, so why change it?" They are principled and industrious, and they often struggle with perfectionism due to their high ideals.

All of us can struggle with limiting beliefs. However, Type Ones have a constant inner critic with standards they try to live up to. Their Center of Intelligence is the Body, which means their core emotion is anger. Since openly expressing anger rarely seems appropriate to many Ones, they tend to be at odds with this emotion. They may try to ignore it, but then experience it in criticizing themselves or others.

Emotional Passion: Anger

When in personality, Type Ones experience anger as their primary emotional driver. However, they are often unaware of how their anger truly drives them, and they usually repress it. For Ones, anger rarely looks explosive; instead, it can appear as criticism, perfectionism, resentment, negative self-talk, or outwardly expressed irritation and even disgust. Since Ones like to be seen as appropriate and self-controlled, anger does not feel like an acceptable emotion in most situations. Repression of anger causes it to build, then leak out, rather than be expressed in a healthy manner. This tendency may influence their relationship with money in several ways, leading Ones to express judgment, frustration, resentment, or control surrounding their finances.

Challenges with Money

Money Belief: There's a right way to save money.

Potential Problem/Negative Edge: Rigidity and commitment to money decisions may lead to poor outcomes.

Inflexible, black-and-white thinking can cause problems for Type Ones with their money. These qualities sometimes lead to self-criticism and criticism of others. Other consequences include resistance to change, even while recognizing that money is ever changing. Therefore, Enneagram Ones may be likely to experience sunk cost fallacy—the phenomenon of hesitating to abandon or change a money decision out of diligence and commitment, even when a new direction might be in their best interest. Their commitment to embracing only one way to manage money could present problems such as poor investments, lack of a diverse portfolio, or difficulties pivoting when money must be spent in ways that weren't the original plan.

Most Likely Money Script: Money Vigilance

Themes of the Type One Money Story

- I'm great at money (or I'm not good with my money).
- I'm strict with my budget (or I get sidetracked with my budget).
- I feel great when I have a lot of money.
- I feel upset and discouraged when there's not enough money.
- I set unrealistic expectations for myself and others about money.
- I don't like conversations about money.
- I find myself being critical of others and their money choices.
- My inner critic is pretty severe about my money choices.

- I have zero tolerance for debt but may still have it.
- I want to control my money.

Subtypes and Money

Self-Preservation

Self-Preservation Ones are drawn to routines, rules, and details. They are the most likely of all the Type One subtypes to follow regimented budgets and see one right way of managing money. They may struggle with spending for pleasure and feel the need to be "responsible" with every dollar coming in and out. These individuals may experience heightened anxiety surrounding money and therefore may be less likely to spend it on anything they consider unnecessary. Of all three subtypes, Self-Preservation Ones will be the most opinionated and critical of themselves and their relationship with money, possibly experiencing a great deal of guilt if they are not living up to their own expectations.

Elena

Elena has a job in finance. Working in spreadsheets and reports brings her comfort, and part of her decision to work in this industry was a hope that the structure it provided would influence and improve her finances at home. Although Elena keeps a detailed spreadsheet every month of the family spending, she feels anxious or angry when she predicts there should be a certain amount of money left and there isn't. Elena blames her husband, who refuses to stick to a budget and wants to spend the money he earns spontaneously on himself and their kids. Elena is finding herself fixated on the expectation that there will be several hundred dollars left at the end of each month. Her mounting anger is disrupting her sleep and her relationship, to the point that she's seeking support through financial therapy.

Social

Social Ones want to learn the best way to do something and then model that way for others. They want to give back to the community, and they feel a responsibility to help others learn what they now know. Like the other two subtypes, these individuals are regimented and detail oriented, but they may be more inclined than the other subtypes to spend money on improving the world around them. This could manifest as donating to nonprofits, or taking a job that does not pay as well because they feel a sense of loyalty to its cause.

Marta

Marta works in education. She loves teaching the younger generations and contributes her time to cultivate upcoming leaders. She has never made a lot of money in her career, but she is comfortable and has what she needs in life. However, she feels a sense of superiority for having figured out the correct way to live and spend money, and is often frustrated with others who don't agree with her way of thinking. Her friends and family members wish she would become more open to different ways of spending and investing, maybe even consulting with a financial planner. Marta has politely refused. Because she has difficulty seeing another's perspective when it comes to money, she often sees herself as the expert on her finances already.

One-to-One

One-to-One Type Ones have conflicting desires within them. While the Type One personality urges them to be perfectionistic and rigid, the One-to-One instinct drives them to focus their energy on perfecting others. This is the countertype of the three Type One subtypes. The One-to-One instinct may make this subtype, more than the other One subtypes, likely to spend money on things they want rather than on things they feel they should. Since they have high expectations for not only themselves but the world around them, these individuals are idealists and may struggle with facing and owning the reality of their money situations. They may want to blame others for their financial problems, or reform other people in an effort to fix their own struggles with money.

Paul

Paul is a nurse. He loves helping improve the lives of the people he works with and has never been extremely motivated to make a lot of money. In his view, he has lived a balanced life. Paul works, but he also takes trips around the world to experience new things, and he enjoys some of the finer things in life while doing so. With retirement approaching, Paul is feeling stressed about some of his past money decisions. He realizes he has been distracted by helping other people to the extent that he was not focused on himself. He sees how he has been more impulsive with spending than he was previously aware of, which creates a sense of guilt that he would rather avoid. Paul often feels angry and wanting to blame his partner for lacking boundaries with their budget. He wants to seek support in this area to reduce his anger and guilt, so he reaches out to a financial therapist for help.

Healing and Money
Positive Enneagram Edges/Strengths: Intentional and thoughtful with money, strong money management, consistent and detail oriented
Motivating Money Script: Money Harmony

Elena
Elena expects to have a certain number of dollars at the end of the month, and she realizes this is hurting her more than helping her. It's breeding resentment in her marriage, and it's causing conflict every time her husband wants to do something on the weekend as a family. Elena works hard to recognize that money has movement to it. She identifies imagery of an ocean tide while saying to herself, "When money goes out, it also comes back in."

Elena is developing emotional regulation skills for speaking her worries to her spouse, and she now returns to her values when thinking about spending and saving as a family. She is excited when she's offered a raise several months after working on her money story, and wants to approach things differently with these extra funds.

Marta
Marta realizes that although she is making some really good decisions with her money currently, her unwillingness to acknowledge different, even good, ways of spending and saving has kept her stuck. She agrees to meet with a financial planner, who helps her see additional ways to maximize her portfolio and generate wealth for herself. She is excited to learn about these possibilities because of her love for her family and the idea that she could give back to the youngest generations thanks to her hard work.

Marta is working toward keeping an open mind about how she utilizes her resources, especially as she explores her comfort with taking investment risks. She is curious and asks questions of others so she can continue learning and leaning into her discomfort. When she feels her frustration about money rise up within herself, Marta is able to practice breathing exercises while stating that money has energy, releasing some of the perfectionism she has held on to for so long.

Paul

After starting sessions with a financial therapist, Paul wants to focus on his spending habits. He wants to see where he can create new boundaries rather than allowing his spending to go unchecked. He is learning to show himself compassion in areas where he has been impulsive in the past, without feeling the same crushing sense of guilt.

Paul feels responsible for his future money choices, which for the first time feels empowering rather than overwhelming. He is operating from a spending plan, and has practiced more restraint than ever before, which is building his self-trust. Paul has been using therapeutic techniques to manage his anger, and he and his wife are calmly communicating about their goals to help each other work toward retirement. With his partner's support, Paul recognizes that there is a flow to money, allowing space for enjoying immediate pleasures and supporting long-term goals for their financial future as a couple.

Chapter

Enneagram Twos and Money

Enneagram Type Two is sometimes referred to as The Helper. People with this type hold an internal belief that they are good and okay if they are in proximity to others and helping them, because they will receive love in return. This belief reinforces a core motivation of "I want to be loved." Type Twos are warm and empathetic, often noticing the emotions of others more than their own feelings. It's no surprise that these individuals often seek caregiver roles personally and professionally. They gravitate toward careers such as educator, nurse, physical therapist, occupational therapist, social worker, or psychotherapist to shine as empathetic, available helpers. Although they enjoy helping others, they care more about maintaining connection and being valued than they do about simply helping. Their Center of Intelligence is the Heart, so they interpret the world around them through emotional intelligence and feelings. Because of this, Twos may be prone to emotional spending.

Emotional Passion: Pride

When in personality, Twos experience a sense of pride that causes them to feel as though they know what everyone around them needs, while also thinking that they don't need anything from anyone else. This is a blind spot for many Twos—they often see themselves as wanting to help other people and meet their needs, but fail to recognize that this impulse stems from pride. Concerning money, Twos may use finances to fuel their pride by taking care of other people or refraining from asking for help when they are in need of money. They may use money to gain approval or love, buying gifts for others or for themselves as a way to feel comfort.

Challenges with Money

Money Belief: I must give my time or my money to serve others so that other people love and need me.

Potential Problem/Negative Edge: Financial dependence in self or others may result.

Enneagram Twos have a need to be liked. Other people tend to like those who are helpful, so Twos sometimes help as to attain positive connections with others. Providing funds to loved ones, strangers, or even nonprofit causes can reinforce their desire to be financially supportive and thus valuable to others.

Some Twos feel entitled to the money they earn. For example, if they give their time to a nonprofit or cause they believe in, they may feel even more possessive of their money. Twos' generosity could become a target for manipulation or dependence from others because of their willingness to follow through when helping others in need. This may lead to a struggle with saving for their own futures if they want to assist others with their financial goals.

Most Likely Money Script: Money Avoidance

Themes of the Type Two Money Story
- I experience discomfort with money.
- I am fearful, frustrated, or confused about money.
- I avoid money.
- I struggle to create or stick to a budget.
- I prefer to bill an entity over a person (insurance over private pay).
- Money wasn't spoken about growing up.
- I don't want to be seen as a sellout or greedy when it comes to money.
- I do things to be helpful, not because they are profitable.
- I struggle to raise my rates.
- I suffer from exhaustion and burnout.

Subtypes and Money

Self-Preservation

Self-Preservation Type Twos have conflicting energies within them. While they desire to connect with others and be liked (like all Twos), the Self-Preservation instinct makes them somewhat fearful of this connection. As the countertype of the Type Two subtypes, this Two may be more selective in their willingness to offer support. Although these Twos can be independent and skilled at taking care of themselves, they have a deep, often unconscious, desire to be taken care of. Consequently, they can be ambivalent about close relationships.

It's not surprising that these Twos have a conflicted relationship with money. They want to save money and have financial security, but they may also be waiting for someone else to help them decide how best to do this, or to do it for them entirely. These Twos may even become dependent on another person in an effort to avoid worrying about money altogether.

Kelsey

Kelsey is a mental health therapist who recently moved from an agency to her own private practice. She's decided to panel with insurance to help as many people as she can. However, she struggles financially due to the growing pains of running a small business. Kelsey recognizes that private practice has a whole new learning curve. She determines she must face her money head on in order to make significant changes to her professional and personal finances. She looks for someone she can work well with so she can change things for the better.

Social

Social Twos are often ambitious and driven. They work hard to reach important positions, including leadership roles. While these Twos still want to be helpful and to be liked, they may go about meeting these needs through influence in their communities. This may take the form of giving their time and money to further important causes. While this generous Type Two genuinely wants to help others, they may struggle with noble poverty. Like all the Type Two subtypes, this

Two may not see how their unconscious need to be liked is driving their financial decisions.

Caroline

Caroline works for a nonprofit. While she has never made a lot of money, she has been committed to this organization for many years and is currently its president. Deep down, Caroline experiences a sense of pride for the work she does, as well as for her modest lifestyle. Though frugal, Caroline has accrued a fair amount of debt over the years. She does not want to engage with the reality of her money situation because it makes her feel vulnerable. It even creates a sense of shame that she usually does not have to feel, especially given her success at work. Now Caroline is at a point in her life where she wants to face her money struggles to reduce her debt, and a trusted colleague recommends a financial therapist for support.

One-to-One

One-to-One Twos have a strong desire to connect with others. They share the core Type Two motivation of wanting to be liked, and the sexual instinct further intensifies the need for a strong connection with another person. These Twos may be the most likely of the subtypes to defer to their significant others' money management styles. While all Twos can be somewhat hedonistic, this subtype tends to be the most self-indulgent, with a strong desire to experience life and the pleasures it can bring. This might cause One-to-One Twos to struggle with their spending habits, leaving them in precarious financial situations and looking to someone else to help them out.

Steven

Steven works in sales. His engaging and charming personality has brought him some success in his career. However, he is very generous, and he struggles with spending to the point that he is not financially secure. For many years, he has avoided looking at his bank account. He does not like to face the reality of his financial situation. Steven's partner has tried helping him with a budget, but he struggles to stick with it and often feels constrained by its parameters. He has been trapped in a cycle where he will be disciplined for a time, but then wants to rebel against the system or reward himself by purchasing an expensive want, bringing him back to where he started. Steven is aware of these patterns and wants to create more balance in his relationship with money.

Healing and Money
Positive Enneagram Edges/Strengths: Type Twos are generous and not controlled by money. Financial resources support their goals of connection.

Motivating Money Script: Money Harmony

Kelsey
After attempting to track her income and expenses on her own, Kelsey determines she needs to hire an accountant. She recognizes she isn't consistent enough without the accountability of someone asking her for numbers every month, and the numbers she's seeing in her Electronic Health Record don't appear accurate.

With compassion and trust from her accountant, Kelsey learns that she's been missing expenses and needs to adopt a new system for tracking her numbers. Once she gets through the growing pains of learning something new, Kelsey is excited to see patterns of money flow each month. She is noticing changes in earnings and expenses, as well as a climbing income, as her caseload of clients grows. Although having an accountant was necessary at first, she is now taking ownership of her finances and stepping into her own authority in her relationship with money.

Caroline
After meeting with the financial therapist, Caroline better understands the reasons behind her struggles with money. Growing up, Caroline always wanted to make a significant difference in the world. She now recognizes that her desire to influence the world for the better has created a sense of superiority, which has caused her to feel justified in her spending, as well as her debt.

Caroline is working on her own sense of worth, realizing that she's always had what she needed within her instead of requiring validation from others. She is showing compassion in her self-talk while also making adjustments, so she uses more discretion when offering financial support to others.

Steven

Steven has been working diligently to improve his relationship with money. Having identified his top values as generosity and fun, he has worked those categories into his budget so he can spend with more intention while also establishing better boundaries. Steven is learning about the concept of deprivation, realizing that this feeling has driven his spending habits and emotional spending at different times throughout his life. With the goal of avoiding deprivation, he has learned he can experience more freedom within his budget than he previously did, all while living within his means to feel financially stable. Steven actively reminds himself that money comes and goes, focusing on the steady flow he's created instead of the previous extremes he'd been observing in his finances.

Chapter

Enneagram Threes and Money

Enneagram Type Three is sometimes referred to as The Achiever. People with this type hold an internal belief that they are good and okay if they are successful and others admire them, reinforcing a core motivation of "I want to be approved of." With this in mind, Threes can struggle with vanity, ego, and shape-shifting in order to be seen in a positive light. They fear failure and feel like there is always more they can do. These qualities make them prone to workaholism, as they want to ensure they achieve the success they seek. Although their Center of Intelligence is the Heart, they often struggle to identify and process their emotions, leaving them disconnected from themselves.

Emotional Passion: Self-Deceit

When in personality, Type Threes experience self-deceit as the primary driver in their decisions and relationships. Threes often project an image of success into every scenario they encounter. They naturally become that image, which ultimately leaves them disconnected from their true selves. This is why people may perceive Threes as "chameleons" adapting to their environment. In general, Threes see money as a representation of success, freedom, and security. Depending on the subtype, some may want money to obtain more assets or make themselves more beautiful, while others may stockpile it in order to feel safe. For many Threes, money is a major motivator and area of focus within their lives.

Challenges with Money

Money Belief: I must make more money to be seen as successful.

Potential Problems: Threes may experience workaholism, derive limited joy from money, or feel that money controls them.

Enneagram Threes may have a difficult time separating their self-worth from their net worth. Their success is measured by what they do and accomplish, so making more money indicates greater success in their own eyes and in the eyes of others. This belief encourages workaholism, poor boundaries, and a hustle mentality. Threes can also struggle to find joy in money due to their focus on making more of it. It is common for people of this type to feel they are controlled by money because they are constantly ruminating on how much they are making, by what means, and how often.

Most Likely Money Script: Money Focus

Themes of the Type Three Money Story

- I don't want to think about money because it makes me feel bad.
- I feel controlled by money.
- My success is wrapped up in how much money I make.
- I can always work more to make more money.
- There is never enough money (scarcity).
- I fear I don't know how to make the most of my money.
- I want to take educated, calculated risks when investing my money.
- Debt is a personal failure with my money.
- I cannot make mistakes with my money.
- I want to learn how to have my money work for me.

Subtypes and Money

Self-Preservation

Self-Preservation Threes may feel conflicted about their relationship with money. As the countertype of the Type Threes, they present differently in their core motivation, which impacts how they show up in other areas, like money management. This is a Three that not only needs to look good, but also needs to be good.

The Self-Preservation instinct amplifies the Three's need for material security; as a result, this is potentially the hardest working type and subtype on the whole Enneagram. This instinct also sets up the Self-Preservation Three to be one of the most anxious types and subtypes when it comes to money. Although people with this subtype have a strong need to make money and provide for themselves and their families, they are not "showy" because that would go against their desire to "be good." Consequently, their workaholism may be the only outward clue of how driven they are by money and security. For example, this type and subtype may be able to afford the expensive house and car, but they may choose to live in a modest house and drive an unassuming vehicle.

Lana

Lana works all the time in her private practice. Her son complains that he sees her only a handful of hours a week because she starts so early and comes home late. Lana feels driven to make more and more money so she can be a good provider and a hard worker in the eyes of her community, especially since she is a single parent. Her worries about being stereotyped, paired with her current workaholism, are making it difficult for her to hold her boundaries on the client hours she offers each week. Lana is feeling burned out. At the same time, she recognizes her savings account goalpost keeps climbing, even though she's met the original goal several times over.

Social

This subtype is often driven by material success. Social Threes feel a sense of accomplishment when purchasing expensive and luxurious things to prove their success to themselves and others. They may struggle with money boundaries, and despite their potential success, they may also be more prone to debt to afford the lifestyle they desire or want to portray. Part of this drive for material possessions comes from their desire for approval and praise from other people. As a Social type, these Threes see the world through the eyes of their community, and their drive to be admired fuels their need to keep up with current trends and receive recognition for their successes. Competition is another driving factor for this particular type and subtype. They desire to buy what they want when they want it, and to always have the best that money can buy.

Vivian

Vivian founded a successful healthcare practice that she has run for fifteen years. Though she doesn't make the kind of money she could if she worked in a corporate setting, she is proud of what she does, and she likes being able to pick up more work to make more money when she wants. Although she lives a comfortable life and has what she needs (and more), Vivian still feels "behind" when it comes to her success, mainly because some friends from her school are now much wealthier than she is. Though she loves her work, she questions whether she is on the right track and begins to feel discontent when she spends time with this friend group. She begins to investigate other career options that may provide her with more earning potential, though she isn't sure she really wants to make any career changes.

One-to-One

This subtype is driven by the desire to be successful, like the other Type Three subtypes. However, people of this subtype feel successful when those around them are successful. They focus significant attention on being attractive to the most important people in their lives, and they work hard to help them succeed. One-to-One Threes may look like a Type Two from the outside; what differentiates them is their motivation to be admired and successful. These Threes may struggle with spending money, not only on themselves but on their families as a way of showing love and care. Since they care so much about being attractive to others, this subtype may also be prone to spending on things that make them look good, such as nice clothes, skincare, hair, nails, and cosmetic surgeries.

Ian

Ian is a dietitian who spends his life helping other people feel and look better through nutrition and exercise. He has always wanted to be in a helping profession because of the joy he gets from helping others reach their health and fitness goals. He cares deeply about health and vitality, and wants to always appear as his best self as an example to his clients of what they could achieve.

However, Ian spends a lot of time, money, and energy on his appearance. He would like to find a better balance of saving and feeling like he can still indulge himself from time to time. He wants to create a budget but doesn't know where to start. Ian begins asking close friends and family members about a direction to go, and a trusted friend decides to help him with creating his budget.

Healing and Money

Positive Enneagram Edges/Strengths: Type Threes are skilled at finding ways to earn more money. They are creative and curious about investments and opportunities to invest money, and are interested and eager to learn more about money.

Motivating Money Script: Money Plentiful

Lana

Lana recognizes the irony in her efforts as a parent. In loving her son and wanting to provide for him, she is working so hard that she feels she's failing at being present for him. This reality check has prompted her to hold better boundaries at work. She's also discovering how fatigued she feels when finally slowing down to breathe.

In an effort to prevent further rupture in her relationship with her son and avoid burnout, Lana starts reading financial psychology books to better understand the emotions that drive her money behaviors. While completing a journal prompt about her future relationship with money, Lana realizes she has several concrete measures of future financial success in place. Not only that, but she has already met 90 percent of those money goals in the present!

Since giving herself permission to slow down, Lana has also been addressing some of the underlying emotions that fuel her anxiety to work so hard. She is learning how to engage with these emotions and is feeling less pressure to stay busy, which in turn allows her to be more present with her son.

Vivian

After speaking with a career counselor, Vivian recognizes she is one of the rare people who feels passionate about their work. She loves what she does, and only questions whether she loves it when surrounded by people who make more money than she does.

Rather than change her entire career path to pursue wealth, Vivian surrounds herself with like-minded people who encourage her to feel content with where she is in life. She establishes more boundaries with the friend group that makes more money than she does when it comes to her thoughts and emotions, but she also limits the amount of time she spends with them. Her competitiveness and discontentment drastically decrease as a result of these small changes. Vivian is practicing daily gratitude to remind herself of the success she already has, allowing her to further enjoy her work on a daily basis.

Ian
Ian's friend shares that she created her budget around her core values. She learned this approach through a coaching group and really connected with the idea. Ian identifies his core values are service, health, beauty, relationships, and positivity. Through this exercise, he realizes he has been feeling disconnected from himself and has lost a sense of who he is over the years of working in this industry.

Now, not only is Ian creating a budget based around these core values, but he is also doing the work to get to know himself better. He is starting to focus time on connecting with himself and his deeper emotions rather than always focusing on others like he has in the past. By doing so, Ian is feeling more secure in who he is. He has less of an urge to make himself attractive to others, because he already feels attractive.

Chapter

Enneagram Fours and Money

Enneagram Type Four is sometimes referred to as The Individualist. People with this type hold an internal belief that they are good and okay if they are being uniquely authentic, reinforcing a core motivation of "I want to be significant." Folks who identify as Fours are often creative, artistic, and deeply emotional. They may feel misunderstood by others even though they long to feel connected.

They can easily see what's missing in themselves and within life. They dislike surface-level conversations, preferring deeper discussions for connection and meaning. Their Center of Intelligence is the Heart, and they certainly rely on their feelings to make decisions and interpret the world around them. Like Twos, Fours may be prone to making financial decisions based on emotions.

Emotional Passion: Envy
When in personality, Type Fours experience envy in a variety of ways. This could manifest as comparing themselves to others or to past versions of themselves, focusing on what they don't have, engaging in nostalgic remembrance and longing for the past, or feeling as though they lack something significant.

In terms of money, the passion of envy can drive Fours to long for material possessions they don't yet have, deny themselves things they want due to feelings of unworthiness, or overspend on things they think will bring them happiness or satisfaction. Depending on the subtype, money may or may not be important to Fours. However, for all Fours, money is a means of self-expression stemming from the passion of envy.

Challenges with Money

Money Belief: Money is bad/corrupt AND I envy others who seem happier with more money (so what am I missing?).

Potential Problems: A Four may be an underearner who struggles to meet money goals and might endure poverty (similar to a Two) OR they may seek to be extraordinary or special, potentially desiring envy from others due to status as a high earner (resembling a Three).

Enneagram Fours tend to be feelers and creatives. They enjoy deeper conversations, which can include the topic of how money hurts or helps others. Prior to doing their own money work, they may believe that money is bad or corrupt. This belief can lead to a conscious or subconscious rejection of money, resulting in underearning because they don't want to hold on to money.

Many Fours have a tendency to become overly attached to suffering, and their perception of money is no exception—especially for those in helping professions. They may exist in long suffering about their ability to "go without," or even take pride in the fact that they don't make enough money. They may choose to sit in their melancholy feelings for what they want, but can't afford. But once they do their own money work, Fours can experience a healthy shift from "Money is bad" to "Money is a tool," or some other neutral belief that indicates changes in their relationship with money for the better.

Most Likely Money Script: Money Avoidance or Money Status

Themes of the Type Four Money Story
- I want to feel understood in my money choices.
- I like material things that embody beauty and art, and are of good quality.
- I like to control how I spend and save money.
- I feel anxious when I don't have enough money (or I'd feel better if I had more money).
- I have all the feelings about money.
- I'm either an underearner or an overachiever with my money.
- I don't trust money systems.

- I don't handle unplanned expenses well.
- I never have enough money and other people do.
- Money prevents people from being authentic.

Subtypes and Money

Self-Preservation

Self-Preservation Fours have a conflicted relationship with money. These Fours may look like Enneagram Threes in that they are typically hardworking and high achieving, and they often appear unemotional in the face of challenges. On the one hand, they can make a lot of money through their work ethic, and they may work hard to avoid avoid a sense of needing in their lives.

However, they are the countertypes of the Type Fours. As such, they feel the need to prove their worth independently—by not asking for assistance or complaining along the way. Because some Self-Preservation Fours have the tendency to be long suffering, they may not need much to get by. In this case, they unconsciously choose to live in poverty for the sake of proving they can overcome this challenge. While the Self-Preservation instinct causes them to want security, their propensity to belittle suffering sets them up to be stoic in the face of challenges. As such, they may inadvertently set themselves up for suffering in order to demonstrate perseverance when it comes to money.

Alex

Alex has worked for the same nonprofit organization for fifteen years. From the outside, he appears driven, focused, independent, and unflappable. Inside, however, Alex feels burned out, pressured, lonely, and stuck in a job that he once cared deeply about, but feels no passion for now. He has not received a raise for the past five years and feels that if his superiors thought he deserved one, they would have given it to him. He operates under the belief that if he keeps working hard, the leaders of his nonprofit will recognize his efforts and reward him.

Unfortunately, Alex has not felt happy or at peace in a long time, and work is a major contributing factor to his overall stress level. He wants to feel the passion he once had for his job, and although he longs to feel connected in his life, he is burned out and wary of letting others in. He decides to confide in his brother, who happens to be an Enneagram enthusiast who has some ideas about income.

Social

These Fours have the tendency to focus on their experience of suffering. They are uniquely attuned to their inner longings and often spend time and energy thinking about what is missing. As a result, they sometimes remain steeped in melancholy. Further, they hold the belief that what they need and what is good are both outside themselves. This belief contributes to a feeling that they are lacking in significant ways.

This pattern is familiar and comfortable for Social Fours, who often feel the need to embrace feelings of sadness because when they experience strong emotions, they feel connected and authentic. This Four may be the most outwardly envious of people who have more money than they do. They may also be skeptical of people with money in general because they tend to regard appearances as fake or inauthentic.

Jarelle

Jarelle loves collecting intricate art for her office and home spaces. She also invests in custom jewelry that makes a statement and leaves an impression on her clients. Although Jarelle enjoys beautiful things, she has a deep mistrust of people with a significant amount of money, assuming they are inauthentic and greedy. When Jarelle works with clients who disclose they have wealth or are high-income earners, she feels an immediate desire to withdraw. This tendency worries her because she wants to show up authentically alongside her clients.

One-to-One

The One-to-One Four may struggle with excessive competitiveness when it comes to money. They may look at other people who have more money than they do and try to become superior as a way to exceed their peers' success. They may think that people who have more money are better than those who do not have much.

One-to-One Fours may openly want to be seen as extraordinary, so they may eagerly put their home, cars, clothes, and jewelry on display so others feel desire for what they have. They are sometimes aggressive about pursuing their money goals and won't stop until they have what they want. This subtype may also be skeptical of money systems, thinking they are being held back or "put in a box" by traditional forms of managing money.

Kim

Kim finds herself dissatisfied in life. After hustling in her twenties and thirties, she is burned out, irritable, and angry, and she often takes out her emotions on the people closest to her. When she looks at her life, she doesn't understand why she is frustrated because she feels she has a better life than many people. She has a nice home, decent savings, a good job, and the ability to travel with her partner on planned vacations several times a year. Yet Kim finds herself snapping at her loved ones often, which makes her feel out of control.

When her partner gently confronts her about her anger and the way she interacts with her family, Kim realizes she's angry that she pursued a vision of wealth that was fed to her by her parents and society but which hasn't felt authentic to her for years. Realizing she wants things to change, Kim reaches out to a therapist for support.

Healing and Money

Positive Enneagram Edges/Strengths: Fours are good at spending money on things they truly value. They can manage their money diligently and live off little if necessary, and they easily understand the depth of emotions associated with money.

Motivating Money Script: Money Optimism

Alex

Alex's brother helps him see how his subtype is reinforcing some money behaviors. As the countertype of the Type Four group, Alex has a tendency to keep himself in difficult situations without recognizing that he's doing it. Since the conversation with his brother, he has noticed how his personality patterns have kept him stuck in this misery when, in reality, he's had the power to change his situation the whole time.

Through some deep self-reflection and some education from his brother, Alex is starting to get out of his own way. He has even decided to meet with a coach who specializes in salary negotiation within nonprofits. This experience has given Alex some confidence and language for advocating for a raise, while also providing him the safe space to work on money mindset shifts about his worth at work.

Jarelle

Jarelle seeks the help of a financial therapist after learning about financial therapy on a healer podcast. She's excited to work with someone who wants to talk about the deep feelings of money, and comes into the work fully present. Jarelle discovers some financial trauma in her family tree around wealth and estrangement, which is contributing to her current beliefs about wealth being a sign of greed and inauthenticity. Through some hard work, Jarelle transforms her money beliefs from negative to neutral, allowing herself to engage her clients from a place of curiosity and compassion.

Kim

Kim works hard in therapy to address the years of anger she's felt. Through this process, she realizes that her anger is connected to her thoughts and feelings about wealth and work-life balance. Kim recognizes that her anger can be a helpful guide toward living in her values and desires, though she continues to work on expressing her anger in healthier ways. She understands that her competitiveness is a strength when it comes to personal finances because she can channel it into being self-competitive. Additionally, she is actively working on the way she compares herself to others, which has historically driven her toward success. Kim begins to feel at peace with where she is in life, believing she already has everything she needs to feel fulfilled.

Chapter

Enneagram Fives and Money

Enneagram Type Five is sometimes referred to as The Investigator. Type Fives hold an internal belief that they are good and okay if they have enough resources and are competent. Often, they feel capable and safe when gaining knowledge, researching, observing, and holding on to what they have, which reinforces a core motivation of "I want to protect my time and energy." Because they fear being depleted of resources, Fives are private people who like their space and are overwhelmed by too much emotion. Their Center of Intelligence is in the Head. As such, they believe knowledge is power. They go all in when exploring something they are passionate about. Sometimes they fail to act because they want to gain more knowledge to feel fully prepared.

Emotional Passion: Avarice

When in personality, Type Fives are driven by a fear that they will not have enough resources; therefore, they believe they must conserve what they have. While avarice may be traditionally defined as "greed," Fives are not greedy for material possessions as much as they are stingy with what they already have.

In many cases, Fives live minimalist lives, thinking that they can get by on little and denying themselves excess resources. Money is no exception—most Fives know how to stretch a dollar and will contemplate the value of something before they spend money on it.

However, for things that are important to a Five, they usually want quality and will spend in a way that sets them up to receive the most long-term benefits from their purchases and investments.

Challenges with Money

Money Belief: I must master money and how to invest it AND I worry that while I don't need much, I also don't have enough.

Potential Problems: Fives may lack a full understanding of the emotional components of money in themselves and others. They may hoard money or, conversely, live off next to nothing.

Enneagram Fives tend to be logical, left-brained individuals. They may invest time and funds into educating themselves on money matters, including investments and the stock market. Some Fives track money as if it were a job, with a serious commitment to checking their numbers or consuming financial news daily.

Because of their focus on how money works, Enneagram Fives may miss opportunities to understand the psychology of money in themselves and others, assuming the emotional decisions of others are impulsive or irrational. Further, because of their fixation on resources, Fives may also oscillate between fearing they don't have enough money and hanging on to their resources too tightly. Alternatively, they may be driven by a sense of frugality that causes them to lead miserly lives and believe that they don't need much. This tendency often results in missed opportunities to make the most of their money.

Most Likely Money Script: Money Vigilance

Themes of the Type Five Money Story
- I have a good sense of budgeting and money management.
- I think I should manage my finances by myself with no help.
- I have a fear of judgment about my money.
- I may have a personal or family history of scarcity.
- I don't like when other people get emotional about money.
- I should know everything about money.
- I don't need much to survive on.
- What course can I take to learn about money?
- I want to feel like there's enough money.
- I want to live in congruence or abundance, not scarcity.
- Subtypes and Money

Self-Preservation

The Self-Preservation Type Five is likely to be frugal and possessive with the money they have. Since Fives already have a leaning toward stinginess, the Self-Preservation instinct fuels this tendency even further. As a result, this subtype experiences a powerful fear that they will run out of resources. While this doesn't mean people of this subtype will be wealthy, it does mean they are protective of what is currently in their possession. And often these Fives do not possess a lot. Even though they may fear not having enough, this type is unlikely to discuss their personal matters with anyone. They tend to be the most guarded of the Type Five subtypes, and possibly of all the subtypes on the Enneagram.

Jody

Jody is one of very few specialists trained in an up-and-coming protocol for chronic pain management. She invested years and dollars into developing competency, and became known in her community as the go-to person for this service across several states. Jody doesn't like the spotlight, but she recognized a need, and she continues to meet that need with quality and efficient care.

Jody wants to increase her financial stability for retirement now that her practice seems overly full. She recently started exploring additional training in her specialty that will cost several more thousands of dollars and require significant travel. Jody has noticed that she is hesitant to invest in the next level of her training due to the cost and losing patient income in her absence. In her mind, she sees her revenue going down instead of up with this expenditure, and that makes her fearful.

Social

The Social instinct makes this subtype of Fives the most likely to want to master money matters. Social Fives have an insatiable desire to gain knowledge in the areas that interest them. In addition to researching, these Fives often learn by collecting information from knowledgeable people in their lives. Their thoughts about money may be idealistic, however, and they may fall into the trap of thinking they are the expert on money. As a result, they may struggle with their finances, partly because they don't foresee money pitfalls in their lives, and also because they don't want to admit that they need help. When they do ask other people about money matters, it often has more to do with their need to be always learning than it does with having humility and a willingness to be teachable.

Kyle

Kyle successfully built a healthcare practice because of his skill in fostering connections with other people. He has been interested in wealth management for a while, and has been surveying colleagues about methods that have helped them succeed with investing and saving for their retirement.

Kyle began exploring this area several years ago. However, he has yet to decide where he will invest his money. He still thinks there might be a better opportunity out there, and he doesn't want to spend time and energy changing all his accounts only to find himself stuck in a less-than-ideal financial situation. Realizing he has been talking about investing for a while but has not been able to start something, Kyle reaches out to a financial adviser for advice on how to maximize his resources. Even as he explores booking an appointment, he notices some worry about whether he will have enough energy to follow through.

One-to-One

The One-to-One Type Five may look more like a Type Four from the outside. While they are consistent with the other two subtypes in how they guard resources, this is the countertype of the Type Five subtypes because of how the One-to-One instinct drives them toward connection to another. Other Fives usually fear this level of intimacy and connection due to how it may drain their energy. However, this Five usually only wants this level of connection with a romantic partner or maybe a few close friends. This subtype needs to fully trust in order to feel connected, but they often require a lot from the other person to achieve this level of trust.

These Fives may struggle to be practical and realistic about money, as they have a tendency toward romanticizing people and possibly their own finances. They also tend toward minimalism like the other Five subtypes; however, this Five may be more likely to desire extravagance in the small quantity of items they possess.

Heather

Heather is an art therapist and loves using her passion for expressing beauty to connect with and help others express themselves. She hasn't prioritized money management in her adult life, and she hasn't seen the need to since she has always had what she needs.

Recently, however, Heather has considered branching off from her community mental health job to start her own practice. Although she desires this change, she fears she will not have what she needs to be a successful art therapist on her own. She feels especially nervous about the benefits loss, the monthly rent, and the supplies she will need to purchase up front. Heather decides to confide in a close friend and colleague she trusts to see if that will help her work through her thoughts and apprehensions.

Healing and Money

Positive Enneagram Edges/Strengths: Type Fives are deliberate in their spending, savvy with saving and investing, good at money management, and willing to increase their knowledge about financial strategies.

Motivating Money Script: Money Plentiful

Jody

Jody comes across financial therapy in her quest to make some decisions about her future. She presents her options for problem solving and learns to get curious about her body sensations in the process. Jody believes she's never approached money from a place of emotions before, and she uncovers some childhood memories that influenced her desire to remain in logic over emotions.

Through the work, Jody learns to tap into her emotions more easily when it comes to money in order to make values-based decisions about her business and her personal money goals. She determines she can postpone and save for the training, so she has the money available up front. She also works with her admin team to streamline her schedule for existing clients, notifying them of her scheduled absence to ensure minimal disruption to her revenue.

Kyle

Although Kyle wants to make a move, his desire to be autonomous is interfering with his ability to start working with a financial adviser.

After another stalled start, his partner gives him three options of people to meet. She asks him to choose one and set a date for a meeting. Kyle and his partner meet with his selected adviser, and Kyle realizes that having begun this process, he has what he needs to make decisions, move money accordingly, and invest in the things he wants for his future.

Kyle determines he had been spending more energy thinking about making these moves than were actually required to act on them. He recognizes how his desire to be self-reliant actually held him back from making more money, starting two years earlier when he began thinking about investing. However, rather than dwelling on what could have been, Kyle acknowledges that moving into action often helps bring clarity to any situation. As a result, he attempts to remain flexible. In working with a financial adviser and his partner, Kyle is building self-confidence and learning to trust that he will have what he needs if and when any financial changes need to occur.

Heather

Heather's friend helps her think through all aspects of branching out to start her own business. After weighing the pros and cons, Heather decides to move forward with starting her own art therapy practice. As part of planning, she identifies the steps she must take before she can quit her community mental health job. Having a concrete plan in place helps reduce her fears and also prepares her for the reality of this transition, especially since she can sometimes struggle to focus on the big picture by getting lost in the details.

Next, Heather takes action on the steps she identified. She starts searching for a place to rent, as well as shop for supplies that are on sale to maximize her budget. Since she has already identified a monthly business budget, Heather will be ready to quit her job when the right practice location comes up. She will feel confident that it's a good fit based on a few simple wish-list items she and her friend came up with for her dream space. Heather now feels hopeful rather than fearful about this upcoming change.

Chapter

Enneagram Sixes and Money

Enneagram Type Six is sometimes referred to as The Loyalist. People with this type hold an internal belief that they are good and okay if they are safe and have support. This often looks like the Six being responsible and doing what's expected of them, which reinforces a core motivation of "I want to be secure." Folks who embody Type Six tend to be vigilant, skeptical, observant, and worried about the various possibilities that may happen in which they have no control. This causes them to doubt or question constantly, resulting in mistrust and decision fatigue.

Authority figures are important to each of the Type Six subtypes, though they will relate to them in unique ways. Although some Sixes will tell you they do not experience anxiety, other people often perceive them as anxious, especially concerning money. Interestingly, Sixes may convey calmness during a financial crisis, as they have already anticipated this stress, and mentally and emotionally prepared for it ahead of time. Sixes' Center of Intelligence is the Head, so they will use strategy and logic to navigate money situations.

Emotional Passion: Fear

When in personality, Type Sixes make many decisions out of fear, even if they do so unconsciously. Fear can manifest in many ways, including indecision or analysis paralysis, skepticism, questioning, worrying, anxiety, self-doubt, or even anger. Money matters are not exempt from the extensive fear found in a Six's personality. Sixes often look for reassurance or security in response to their fear, which may take the form of saving, investing, being frugal, or constantly thinking and worrying about money. The three subtypes of the Enneagram Six are starkly different, however, and their relationship with money varies based on their subtype, especially when it comes to risk tolerance.

Challenges with Money

Money Belief: I must be responsible with my money OR I need money to remain secure.

Potential Problems: Sixes might experience deprivation from focusing solely on saving, and may feel guilt when spending.

Anxiety and analysis paralysis can plague Enneagram Sixes when they are in an unhealthy state, such as when they are worried about money. Sixes may struggle to spend money, fearing consequences or financial emergencies where they wouldn't have enough. They seek to be responsible with their money. Sixes may feel guilt when buying things if they don't have the space to thoroughly analyze the consequences, or when making large purchases that have a significant impact on their budget or bank account. Further, because Sixes have difficulty trusting—both themselves and others—they may struggle to act on purchases they want, questioning their own desire for the item and then agonizing over the choice of whether to purchase.

Most Likely Money Script: Money Focus

Themes of the Type Six Money Story

- I overthink everything and experience analysis paralysis.
- I'm good at playing things through in every scenario.
- I don't feel I have enough money.
- I don't know how much to save for emergencies.
- I'm good at saving money.
- I don't like debt.
- I'll stay in a job if it offers stability.
- I can handle small purchases with minimal anxiety.
- I ruminate over the best money strategies.
- I struggle to take action steps when it comes to my money.

Subtypes and Money

Self-Preservation

The Self-Preservation Six is intensely fearful about money and security. Of all the Type Six subtypes, this one is the most in touch with fear because of how the instinct and the type pair together. As a result, these Sixes often look to an authority figure for guidance and security. They may be the most likely to hire a coach, therapist, or adviser to help them consider all their options. However, they are also the subtype that questions themselves and others the most, so even though they want guidance, they may be doubtful of the advice given and therefore find themselves stuck in decision fatigue regarding their money.

Evonne

Evonne has worked with the same employer for the last seventeen years. Although the work has become monotonous, she feels stuck in her job to maintain financial security for herself and her family. She has experienced several years of little to no bonuses and no raises, which gets her thinking about a possible pivot out of her familiar and oftentimes boring job. Evonne has a decent savings account, but the idea of seeking a new job leaves her anxious and uncomfortable. What if the pay is even less? What if she dislikes it even more? Evonne knows she has to make some decisions, but she feels paralyzed by the possibilities of starting over with a new employer.

Social

Because of the Social instinct, these Sixes want to build a strong community of alliances to consult when making important decisions—including financial ones. They tend to be the most responsible of the subtypes and adhere to a set of standards they can trust, in order to feel more confident. These Sixes enjoy structure, routine, and clearly defined boundaries, often taking it upon themselves to set an example for others. They may be the most likely to follow traditional, low-risk approaches to money management, potentially losing out on opportunities to invest due to their resistance to change and their rigid thinking. They often feel responsible for providing for the people around them, while also struggling to trust or allow others to provide for themselves.

Daniel

Daniel feels a responsibility to the community at large, which is why he has worked in education for the past ten years. He is dedicated to making a difference in students' lives and finds fulfillment in the impact he has as an educator of young minds. Daniel has struggled financially for years and has significant debt that he has been paying down consistently for quite some time. Wanting guidance on how to best navigate his debt on a teacher's salary, Daniel found and adopted a financial advising method early on and has been dedicated to this system for the past decade.

Recently, however, Daniel has grown increasingly tired of his financial situation. He has not allowed himself to spend money on "nonessentials" in years per this financial system's recommendations. He is feeling exhausted and doesn't know how to stop feeling stuck financially. He shares his struggles with his sister, an accountant, who offers to look through his finances and give her input.

One-to-One

This subtype of Six may be the most likely to take money risks. Although these individuals struggle with fear like all Sixes, they would rather confront their fears head on than give in to them, making them the countertypes of the Sixes. The One-to-One instinct brings with it a drive for intensity, and often these Sixes enjoy being in a state of daring excitement. This could be achieved through work, hobbies, relationships, or even finances. Though they can work very hard, this subtype may struggle with managing the money they have due to their impulsive purchases or an attraction to high-risk, high-reward methods.

Rachel

Rachel is an attorney. She has spent a lot of money on her education and cares more about using her skills and knowledge to help people than she does about paying off debt. In her current financial situation, Rachel doesn't like looking at her bank account, continues to spend money on things she wants or finds exciting, and does not want to let anyone else know about her financial reality. At times, she doesn't want to know the reality of her finances herself either.

However, Rachel is in a committed relationship and feels ready to purchase a home with her partner. Unfortunately, her credit has been in bad shape for several years, and she is struggling to qualify for a home loan. Rachel becomes increasingly angry and even aggressive with the people who are working with her and her partner to finance their home.

Healing and Money

Positive Enneagram Edges/Strengths: Sixes are good at saving and investing money. They are detail oriented when it comes to their finances. They tend to optimize savings with they make purchases, and they are unlikely to spend impulsively.

Motivating Money Script: Money Harmony

Evonne

Evonne works with a career coach who came recommended in her friend group. She wants help identifying some career paths that could continue to provide financial stability while also allowing her to feel interested in her work again. Evonne is struck by the coach's simple question: "What if it all worked out?" Playing through that outcome with an absence of anxiety gives Evonne some clarity around her interests and values, helping her narrow down the industries she can explore further for a possible job change when she's ready.

Daniel

Daniel's sister has noticed how disciplined he has been at managing his money over the years. She helps him see that although he feels "stuck" in his situation, his dedication to paying down debt has meant that he is already over 70 percent done with his payments. Daniel realizes he has been so focused on getting out of debt that he has not looked back on what he already accomplished.

Knowing he is almost three quarters of the way toward his goal, Daniel decides he can start to loosen up on his rigid payment plan and begins to save for a vacation to take a much-needed break. While still committed to paying off his debt, Daniel is able to enjoy the process of saving money for himself. He finds he can already experience more freedom just thinking about taking a planned vacation this coming summer.

Rachel

Rachel learns she can channel her aggression into paying down her debt, which is much more productive than using it to show her dissatisfaction about things she cannot control. She recognizes that her anger is a sign of fear, and, with the help of her partner, she engages it. Rather than denying her fear of money, she confronts it head on, using her power and courage to work through the discomfort that it brings.

Rachel is able to show herself compassion for the ways she has denied her financial situation, while also making the necessary changes to get out of unhelpful patterns. Not only that, Rachel is learning to accept help from her partner rather than trying to fix this issue independently. As a result, they both feel more connected, and Rachel is able to practice trust in a new way.

Chapter

Enneagram Sevens and Money

Enneagram Type Seven is sometimes referred to as The Enthusiast. People of this type hold an internal belief that they are good and okay if they are feeling joy and have the freedom to do what they want. They do not like experiencing pain or boredom, reinforcing a core motivation of "I want to be free and happy." Sevens are often extroverted and like to keep their options open. They value creativity, experiences, and autonomy to pursue the things that feel most rewarding to them. As part of the Head Center of Intelligence group, Sevens are quick-minded individuals who often experience rapid-fire thoughts and ideas. They are strategists by nature and are always looking out for the best opportunities. Though most Sevens will not resonate with fear as a core emotion, it manifests for them through a need to avoid pain and sadness rather than a true desire to always experience pleasure.

Emotional Passion: Gluttony

When in personality, Type Sevens have a strong desire to experience variety. They need to have options in order to create and choose the best experiences for themselves. Rather than interpreting gluttony only in the context of food, Sevens have an insatiable need for pleasure, freedom, and fun when their passion is driving their choices. Concerning money, Sevens may see it as a means to achieve this deep desire for the things and experiences they want. This tendency will drive their money decisions unless they are conscious of their personality patterns.

Challenges with Money

Money Belief: I will spend money to feel happy. Having more money or finding good deals I can spend money on will make me happy.

Potential Problems: This type might have limited or no money for retirement or emergencies.

Enneagram Sevens love to live life to the fullest. This may mean pursuing new experiences or seeking dopamine through spending. Other people sometimes view this as chasing the next shiny object, resulting in judgment. Due to their passion and various interests, Sevens can struggle to save enough, whether that's for a vacation next year or retirement in twenty years. They live for the anticipation of joy or reward, which can have a negative effect on their emergency or long-term savings accounts.

Most Likely Money Script: Money Status or Money Focus

Themes of the Type Seven Money Story

- I am comfortable with money.
- I only see the positives of money.
- I like to invest in experiences.
- I'm good at budgeting to get what I want.
- I can get creative in making money goals happen.
- I excel at seeing the global view of spending.
- Money has energy and I want that energy to work for me.
- I can be generous with others who matter to me.
- I live for the anticipation of the next money adventure.

Money is a tool to help me live the life I want.

Subtypes and Money

Self-Preservation

The Self-Preservation Seven thrives on finding the best deals and making the most of their money. As with all the subtypes of Seven, they want to maximize everything in life. Since they share a concern for security and safety with all Self-Preservation subtypes, they often make connections with others who help give them the best options in life—and this includes financial options. Sevens may unconsciously set themselves up for the most success by surrounding themselves with people who manage their own money well and from whom they can benefit in some manner. This Seven will be the most opportunistic when it comes to money, whether that means capitalizing on a good deal or embracing someone else's knowledge when it comes to money management.

Cam

Cam runs a nonprofit organization and has been highly successful at marketing and engaging other people in his business's mission. He prides himself on how he manages money, and considers himself "scrappy" when it comes to stretching a dollar. Despite his effective use of resources, Cam is at a point where he is beginning to feel anxious about his financial security due to inflation and the climbing cost of living. Having made excellent connections over the years through running his organization, Cam reaches out to a financial expert he knows to further address his concerns.

Social

The Social Seven subtype may be the least concerned with spending money on experiences for themselves because their Social instinct causes them to focus on others. While they may be successful with money, they regard showing generosity as more important than spending on themselves. Because they care greatly about bolstering others' feelings of joy and freedom, they may be more likely than the other subtypes to struggle with noble poverty or take jobs that involve sacrificing their time as a resource. This is the countertype of the Seven subtypes, and it may resemble Type Two from the outside.

Remy

Remy is a nurse and has always loved her job helping other people find relief from their pain. She takes pride in living her life in service to others, and although she loves having exciting experiences, she values being generous with her time and resources more than spending money on herself. Because of this, Remy has not taken a true vacation in seven years. She has taken time off here and there for family visits and friends' weddings, but she has always longed to go to France and has never felt like spending that kind of money on a trip.

Recently, Remy has been invited to travel with a friend on a monthlong trip to her dream destination. This feels indulgent and extravagant to Remy, and she doesn't know if she wants to be absent from her job for that long. Remy is feeling the tension between her desires and her practicality and isn't sure what to do.

One-to-One

The One-to-One Seven may be the most optimistic of the already optimistic Seven subtypes. People of this type have a tendency to see the world through rose-colored glasses, and they always envision the best outcome by (sometimes unconsciously) ignoring the negative aspects or challenges that are in front of them. People with this subtype are the most likely to struggle with saving money and may be prone to indulging in positive experiences. In fact, they may not realize the importance of saving money, justifying spending in the here and now because preparing for the future will be their future self's problem. This thought process serves as a way of denying a limitation that they don't want to face. The One-to-One's signature trait of intensity sets them up to desire copious pleasure, and money is a means to that end.

Alexis

Alexis loves investing in experiences, both in her personal and professional life. As a healer new to private practice, she is excited to further fund her lifestyle and increase the possibility of meaningful experiences outside of client work. Alexis struggles to save for retirement when there are opportunities to spend on experiences that improve her life in the present.

She wants self-permission to pursue experiences as they arise, but she also wants the financial freedom a healthy retirement account could provide for her future self. Alexis has a history of being overly optimistic about the future, thinking that the money will be there even if she doesn't change her habits in the present. As time goes on, she realizes that the only way she can work toward the future she truly wants is to make some changes now.

Healing and Money

Positive Enneagram Edges/Strengths: Sevens usually have a positive, healthy relationship with money. They are free from guilt when spending it on things or experiences that bring them joy, and they easily think of new ways to make money when motivated to do so.

Motivating Money Script: Money Optimism

Cam

Cam's colleague pores over his financials and points out several areas that need Cam's attention. Cam admits he might have been avoiding money matters at this deeper level due to his desire to avoid pain; he has dreaded confirming that his numbers aren't where they should be. Cam works to engage with the reality of his company's situation and practices tolerating the accompanying stress. He also practices visualizing where his company will be when he comes out on the other side of these challenges, an exercise that allows him to see success. With healthier books, Cam discovers he can engage in even more generosity through his business, because he is not worried about his own security. As a result, his organization can expand even further and allow Cam to experience financial freedom in his business and personal life.

Remy

Remy has been working with a therapist for a few months to manage the anxiety that has surfaced. Through this work, she has identified some difficult experiences that she hasn't fully processed. Remy notices that a big factor in her desire to help other people stems from an unconscious need to avoid pain and help others do likewise. Remy's therapist also helps her see she can learn to develop healthy boundaries with her work and take better care of herself so she can continue helping people through her job far into the future.

Bearing these things in mind, Remy makes the "selfish" decision to go to France and take a month off work. During this time, she connects with a deeper part of herself that she had not previously known well because she'd lacked the opportunity to slow down. Remy returns from her trip with a greater awareness of her own needs, not just the needs of others. Although her vacation was a big expense, Remy realizes that spending money on herself is important, especially if it increases her ability to be there for others more fully.

Alexis

Alexis decides to work with a financial coach as she builds up her private practice, hoping the experience will anchor her in some money decisions that focus on her future. The financial coach recognizes Alexis's motivators and creativity, inviting her to gamify some of her savings to see if it brings more excitement and joy. Alexis decides to invite her friends into a money-saving challenge that is playful and rewarding. She finds herself connecting more deeply with friends in the experience of saving while also seeing her numbers grow, a pleasurable combination that motivates her to continue balancing the two within her life.

Chapter

Enneagram Eights and Money

Enneagram Type Eight is sometimes referred to as The Challenger. People with this type hold an internal belief that they are good and okay if they are strong and lead the charge in any given situation, reinforcing a core motivation of "I want to be in control." Enneagram Eights have big energy when they enter a room, and they connect to themselves and others through passion and intensity. They tend to assume a leadership role in many situations, including with spouses or partners or within the workplace. They have a strong sense of justice and often seek to create order and make things right if a situation is within their control. They tend to deny their weaknesses and often ignore their limitations.

Eights have easier access to their anger than the other types, which can cause them to be reactionary rather than rational at times. Since the Body is their Center of Intelligence, Eights are focused on energy and action. With money, this manifests as wanting to do something, whether that means spending more or sticking to a savings plan.

Emotional Passion: Lust
When in personality, Type Eights have a belief that "anything worth doing is worth doing with gusto." Although lust usually has a sexual connotation, the Eight's passion is not always sexual and has a much broader reach. Eights have a tendency to intensely throw their energy into whatever it is that they care about. Fueled by this passion, they

can be excessive in how they engage with their interests. Simply put, lust drives them to want more.

For some of the Eight subtypes, this applies to money and material things as well. Lust may cause Eights to desire immediate gratification, fueling their ability to pursue what they want with unrelenting focus and determination, as well as with money and what it can provide.

Challenges with Money

Money Belief: I will do what I want with my money.

Potential Problems: Conflict in relationships may occur due to the Eight wanting sole decision-making around money. Financial gatekeeping can be an issue.

Enneagram Eights don't like to be told what to do, so to suggest that they save, spend, or use their money a certain way doesn't bode well. Eights like to be the boss, a role that may extend to managing the money in a business or interacting with their partner and family. Their passionate personalities spur them to want to be in the driver's seat when it comes to money. This tendency puts them at risk of financial gatekeeping and often results in conflict with a partner or spouse.

Eights tend to deny their vulnerabilities, so they are likely to have a blind spot when it comes to money weaknesses. Additionally, they can be excessive in their desires, behaviors, and emotions, and money is no exception. They may go to either extreme when it comes to spending and saving, depending on their subtype. Eights don't like rules, so they may reject traditional money systems or norms in order to walk their own path.

Most Likely Money Script: Money Focus or Money Status

Themes of the Type Eight Money Story
- I can be all or nothing in my thinking about money.
- I feel excitement when I have money, and avoidance when I don't.
- I feel energized when thinking about making more money.
- I like working for myself as a small business owner or entrepreneur.
- Money can give me back time-freedom.
- I believe money is a resource I can tap into.

- I've spent money when in my emotions.
- I want my partner or spouse to be on the same page about money.
- I believe I should make the money decisions in our family.
- I want to feel in control of my money.

Subtypes and Money

Self-Preservation
The Self-Preservation Eight is the most guarded of the Type Eight subtypes and has a strong desire for self-protection. People of this subtype find it difficult to trust others, and they are particularly uncomfortable with sharing their vulnerabilities. As with many of the Self-Preservation subtypes, these Eights are practical and go directly after what they want in order to meet their own needs. This subtype is the most concerned with material security and will likely be good at saving money. However, they may not see how their desire for material resources actually keeps them limited.

Karina
Karina has big dreams for her business. She sets goals that will result in higher earnings this year. She wants to invest in systems that will give her back the time-freedom and financial security she has craved for herself as an entrepreneur, wife, and mother. Although Karina is excited about her future, she finds herself frustrated when unexpected expenses pop up. These situations make her feel like she isn't making enough progress, and she responds by trying to exert control over her family or her business. This reaction naturally leads to increased conflict and more resentment within her relationships.

Social
The Social Eight wants to use their power and influence to help protect others. This is the countertype of the Type Eight subtypes. From the outside, people of this subtype may resemble a Social Two because they devote attention to the needs of others. However, they typically focus on protecting others' vulnerabilities rather than helping them as a Two might do. Regarding money, these Eights may be generous with their resources and time in order to further a group, such as

their family or their organization. They may be disconnected from their own needs in favor of the needs of others, so it's important for them to identify and connect with their own vulnerability so they can truly identify what they want and need.

Liz

Liz is a public defender who is passionate about being a voice for the voiceless. She takes pride in her work, and although she doesn't make the type of money she should as an attorney, she loves how she spends her days. Liz exudes passion in everything she does, including in her personal life. She loves to travel, eat out, experience new things, and lavish her friends and family with generous gifts.

The people closest to Liz have expressed worry about her lack of savings, though she has historically ignored these concerns. Recently, though, Liz has been engaging in deeper inner work. She recognizes she could benefit from letting other people help guide her in life, even though she is typically the one with the answers. Money is the area that multiple people have brought up, so she seeks advice about how she can improve her saving habits.

One-to-One

The One-to-One Eight will likely be the most "rebellious" when it comes to traditional ways of managing money. These Eights are passionate, emotional, indulgent, and possessive. They are instinctual in that they want what they want, when they want it. They are the most likely, maybe of all the twenty-seven subtypes on the Enneagram, to struggle with spending money, as they have a tendency to act from impulse rather than after contemplation. Money is a means to experience "more," whether that takes the form of feelings of freedom or an attempt to satiate their desire for intense experiences.

Zeke

Zeke works in education. He leads the theater department in addition to teaching logic and rhetoric to high school students. He loves his job and takes pride in teaching others to better express themselves in both artistic and academic ways. Zeke's passion does not stop with teaching, however. He gives one hundred percent to everything he is involved in and has recently become interested in auto racing.

Besides the car, mechanical repairs, tires, and insurance, Zeke is also responsible for race entries. He has been entering races weekly this season and is accruing quite a bit of debt in the process. He loves this sport and feels too invested and passionate about it to give it up, but he also knows he cannot afford to keep going at his current pace with these races. Zeke feels stuck between his passion and his logic, and he decides to confide in a close friend about his struggle.

Healing and Money

Positive Enneagram Edges/Strengths: Enneagram Eights can create and execute plans to make money when necessary. They can be extremely disciplined with money management while remaining generous toward their inner circle.

Motivating Money Script: Money Plentiful

Karina

Karina decides to get out of her comfort zone and connect with a select few small business owners to identify new ideas for streamlining her business. By working on her money mindset, she learns to tap into her deeper intuition on money decisions, while backing them with facts and figures to help her feel more in control. Karina realizes her need for control is hurting her marriage, so she starts having regular money meetings with her spouse to identify and work toward a shared financial goal. These meetings are pleasurable for Karina, who feels more connected and emotionally aligned with her spouse than before.

She realizes that her fear of not having enough resources has been a driving force in her money decisions, causing her to respond with control rather than getting in touch with the deeper emotions underneath her anger. While this feels incredibly vulnerable to her, Karina experiences a different kind of freedom when she shares this revelation with her spouse.

Liz

Liz finds herself in a financial therapist's office to work on her savings. However, as her therapist invites her to continue her deeper work, she discovers that is initially unrelated to saving skills. She learns that her chosen profession of giving voice to people who feel unheard is a reflection of her financial trauma, as she didn't have a say in her adolescent years about the money she earned. Instead of being able to spend it on what she wanted, her parents expected she would help keep the family afloat financially while her mother was ill.

She also discovers that, although spending money has given her a sense of control, it actually represents rebellion against her mom, who expected so much from her financially at a young age. Liz recognizes that in desiring to be a voice for others, she hasn't learned to put herself first, and she needs to change this to prevent burnout in a career she loves. Healing her relationship with her money can allow her to reframe the relationship she has with saving and spending money as an adult.

Zeke

Zeke's close friend starts by asking questions about his passions from a place of curiosity. It helps that his friend is also a trained financial coach who teaches money strategies for a living. After learning about Zeke's dilemma, his friend asks if he's ever had the experience of saving up for something. Zeke recognizes he lives for the moment and the immediate reward. He is intrigued, however, to learn about research stating that anticipation can be as pleasurable as the reward itself.

With this in mind, Zeke agrees to a money challenge with his friend during the offseason of racing, where he sets money aside to put toward the cost of race entries in the upcoming season. He also does some work around risk, which helps him see that the debt he's accrued has impacted his mental health more than he first realized. Zeke decides to embrace a side hustle to keep him engaged and motivated, which also happens to help him pay off his debt before the next season.

Chapter

Enneagram Nines and Money

Enneagram Type Nine is sometimes referred to as The Mediator. People with this type hold an internal belief that they are good and okay if they are stable and experiencing harmony, both internally and externally. This trait reinforces a core motivation of "I want to be peaceful." Nines often have a blind spot when it comes to their own needs, similar to Twos. They avoid conflict at all costs, and since they don't want to "rock the boat," they don't often speak up about their own needs; this is sometimes because they haven't taken the time to check in with themselves.

They may present as people pleasers to keep the peace, putting themselves at risk of losing a sense of purpose, meaning, and identity that is truly their own. Their Center of Intelligence is the Body, and they are aware of energy and action, though for them, their passion often results in a lack of it.

Emotional Passion: Sloth
When in personality, Type Nines are driven by a desire to have comfort and keep other people comfortable or harmonious, which often results in the Nine's inaction. An important distinction is that, for Nines, sloth is not defined as true laziness. While Nines are busy and motivated people, they can miss the most important action that they need to take, often because they are unaware of their own needs and desires. Concerning money, sloth may cause Nines to remain

stagnant rather than taking important steps with their finances, or they may not know what they want with money, leading to an avoidance of it altogether.

Challenges with Money
Money Belief: Money upsets people, so we don't have to talk about it.

Potential Problems: This type may struggle with money avoidance or accumulating debt.

Due to their natural role as mediators and a tendency to ignore their own wants and needs, Enneagram Nines rarely speak up for themselves. They are at risk of blending with a partner's or family member's wants and needs rather than taking time to identify their own. Each of the three subtypes fights against a tendency to overly attach to a person or a set of values to the point that they lose themselves. Their primary goal is to see all sides of an issue and to help keep the peace.

Since money is a hot button issue for many people, Nines are more likely to avoid talking about it, encouraging avoidance to prevent conflict. This can lead to problems that more frequent discussion could alleviate, including increasing debt, poor money management, and a lack of clarity about the financial future. However, Nines are not doormats—they are likely to respond with stubbornness or passive aggressiveness if they disagree with money decisions. Nines are generally optimistic and may choose to see the positive side of money rather than fully engage with its challenges.

Most Likely Money Script: Money Avoidance

Themes of the Type Nine Money Story
- I feel stressed and frustrated by money.
- I want to avoid money; let's not talk about it.
- I can be thrifty with my money.
- I struggle to move on bigger purchases.
- I want things to last so I don't have to buy them again anytime soon.
- I go along to get along with others on spending.
- I won't bring it up if you owe me money.
- If you say it's a good money practice, I'll follow through.
- I don't want to feel dread or stress about money.
- I want to make enough money to feel comfortable/peaceful.

Subtypes and Money

Self-Preservation

Self-Preservation Nines are the most likely to attach to routines, physical comforts, and practical methodologies. They tend to maintain their budgets because they identify as frugal and want to save. However, their love of creature comforts may make them prone to spending money on things that bring them peace, like self-care treatments, gyms, foods that follow a particular diet, or products that help them feel more relaxed.

These Nines are practical, concrete thinkers who like to keep consistent regimens. They may have difficulty shifting their money mindset, as it feels like a lot of work and they don't want to be told what to do. This subtype is the least likely of the Nines to go along with a partner when it comes to money decisions.

Timothy

Timothy is a healthcare professional who prides himself on being frugal. He desires a simple life and only spends money on himself when it relates to his hobby of running. Although he prioritizes his diet, he is disciplined with his grocery budget each week and regards organic or high-priced foods as indulgences, and therefore unnecessary. The few times his partner (they/them) has purchased foods at higher prices, Timothy has experienced resentment at their inability to stick to the plan and the budget. His partner has asked him repeatedly to branch out of his routine so they can have more variety in their lives, but they are met with resistance or are brushed aside when they bring it up to Timothy. His partner is concerned that they are growing apart, and has asked Timothy to join them in couples therapy.

Social

Social Nines are generally energetic, hardworking, pleasant people. They tend to attach to with the needs of the group or organization with which they associate. As the countertype of the Nine subtypes, they may not look like a Nine from the outside due to the energy they devote to work. They may resemble a Type Three; however, they tend to appear more peaceful. When it comes to money, these Nines may be quite successful, although they are typically motivated by serving others rather than by making money for themselves. They are more outspoken than the other Nine subtypes and may have more opinions on how to manage and spend money, although again, they are more likely to want to serve others with their resources than to accumulate wealth.

Rachelle

Rachelle has worked in a nonprofit as a social worker for almost twelve years. Recently, while helping write up a grant proposal, she saw the budget and payroll of other providers in her workplace. Rachelle was surprised that colleagues with her same training and background were making more money than her, but she didn't plan to say anything, as she didn't want to sound greedy.

While completing her continued education course with a social work colleague, she learned the term "noble poverty" and was struck by how it fit her circumstance with her employer. Rachelle's friend encouraged her to bring back what she learned to her nonprofit to see if any changes could be made that would improve the financial health and wellness of the entire team.

One-to-One

One-to-One Nines are the most likely subtype to attach to a person in proximity to them, whether that's a partner, boss, or close friend. They are agreeable, kind, reserved, and selfless. They may be prone to denying their own wants and needs. As a result, they are likely to avoid having money conversations and spending on themselves, and they might resist setting up long-term savings for the future. Since these Nines tend to struggle with setting boundaries, they may also spend money to the point that they deny the reality of their money situation and overspend.

Lindsey

Lindsey has never thought much about money matters, especially saving for retirement. However, her father recently retired and is struggling to enjoy financial freedom because he did not manage his money well earlier in life. He has advised Lindsey to begin thinking about her own retirement. She searches for some professional advice since she has no experience managing money. Lindsey finds this process overwhelming, but she trusts her father's recommendation and dedicates the time and energy to follow through.

Healing and Money

Positive Enneagram Edges/Strengths: Nines don't put too much pressure on money matters. They are disciplined in sticking to a budget, generous with their money, and deliberate in their financial decision-making.

Motivating Money Script: Money Harmony

Timothy

Timothy is apprehensive but engages in couples therapy, hoping to improve his relationship with his partner. Through the therapeutic work, Timothy recognizes that his resentment is a symptom of failing to communicate his true wants and needs. Until therapy, he didn't fully understand that his anger and unspoken needs were causing him to pull back from a partner who loves him. Now, he is learning new communication skills for speaking up in times of discomfort or distress. Timothy allows himself to adopt flexibility with his partner about spending, including the grocery budget.

Rachelle

When Rachelle shares about noble poverty at work, her message is well received. Her boss, another woman with a master's degree in the nonprofit space, is eager to host conversations with the team about how leadership can show greater appreciation for them, including through financial compensation. Rachelle leaves the conversation inspired to help herself and her team with their financial health, knowing it will support employee retention and the organization's overall mission. With a budget approved, Rachelle's boss tasks her with bringing in a financial therapist trainer who can help her and her colleagues understand the intersection of money and mental health—not just for themselves, but for the populations they serve as an organization.

Lindsey

Lindsey finds a financial adviser through her father and revamps her finances. Initially, she feels a bit lost in the process, as she has really never taken the time to think about what she would want in the future. This process gets below the surface of saving for retirement, motivating her to reevaluate her own wants, hopes, and needs and create a concrete plan for making those goals a reality.

The whole process leaves Lindsey feeling empowered and at peace about the way she spends her money now, since she knows there is a budget and a plan for the present and the future. She also recognizes a new sense of freedom in her spending. For her, it is a relief to work toward a named goal that is uniquely her own.

Chapter

Momentum with Money Healing

How are you feeling about money after reviewing your Enneagram type? Have these reflections motivated you to continue improving your own money story? Now that we've explored your Enneagram edges, it's time to gain momentum in your money healing journey.

Here are three financial therapy exercises with tips for each Enneagram type that can help you take that deeper dive toward meaningful shifts in your money behaviors.

Money Word Association

At the start of this book, we discussed the power that money beliefs have on our financial behaviors. If you've found yourself stuck when trying to identify your money beliefs, consider grabbing a scratch piece of paper or notebook to jot down what you notice as you read each word in this exercise. Writing things down invites you to observe thoughts, feelings, and sensations that are coming up in relation to money.

- Your first word is **savings**.
- Your second word is **debt**.
- Your third word is **credit card**.
- Your fourth word is **wealth**.

What money beliefs are showing up for you as you reflect on the words above? What body sensations? Take this exercise a step further by plotting your beliefs on a spectrum of "good" to "bad" money beliefs. Notice where they land on the line. Notice how many are on one end or the other. Do any of your beliefs feel neutral and land in the middle?

This exercise can provide another layer of self-discovery as you attempt to uncover additional beliefs tied to your past, present, and future relationship with money. To tailor these explorations to your Enneagram type and subtype, be sure to review the added depth questions or suggestions found below.

Ones: Use the spectrum drawing to increase your awareness of black-and-white thinking.

Twos: Challenge yourself to do this exercise on your own first, before considering an accountability buddy.

Threes: Engage in compassionate touch—touch on your body that feels warm and comforting—to embrace vulnerability over success with this exercise.

Fours: Go deeper. Where did your emotions originate? How old are these emotions?

Fives: Using a feelings wheel (found free online) to stay in the emotions longer. What emotions are connected?

Sixes: Contain your anxiety in a real or imagined container so you can engage from true self energy on your own, to start.

Sevens: Anticipate a reward after this exercise to add enjoyment.

Eights: Say your answers out loud. What's it like to hear strength or power in your voice?

Nines: Do this exercise solo. Spread out and take up space.

Self-Preservation: How would it feel to engage with these words from a place of safety? What would it take for you to feel safe? What is standing in your way? Is there anyone else you can depend on to help you reach your goals?

Social: Resist the urge to process with another person. What does it feel like to do this exercise independently? Notice if your mind wants to consider responses to this exercise with a focus on another person rather than yourself. What might you be avoiding that feels difficult to engage with?

One-to-One: How would it feel to view some of these resulting beliefs as helpful guidelines rather than limitations? How does reading these words bring out your competitiveness or rebelliousness? What can you take ownership of iregarding these feelings?

Stacey

Stacey, a mental health therapist and clinical supervisor, engages in the money word association exercise. She identifies stress and anxiety responses for all the words, including "wealth," which catches her by surprise. Through a deeper dive with zero judgment and tons of compassion, Stacey recognizes two primary thoughts waging war within her.

On the one hand, she wants to make a good living for herself and her family. On the other hand, she feels that wealth corrupts people, and she "isn't in (this profession) for the money." Stacey is ready to heal some of her money story to move forward in ways that would help her make a steady income for her financial future while serving populations she is passionate about.

Money Barometer

Imagine you have an amount of money in an account that has no purpose. It's just there. Some readers have an anxiety response just from reading that sentence. "What do you mean it doesn't have a purpose?!" Hang in there, there's more to this exercise. We are going to look at your thoughts and feelings that show up when you consider varying amounts of money in this account with no purpose. Notice what thoughts you have. Notice what reactions come up. Here we go . . .

You have $1,000 in an account with no purpose, it's just there.

Notice what comes up for you. Repeat with the following amounts. Jot down things you are noticing in yourself.

- $5,000 in an account with no purpose, it's just there.
- $10,000 in an account with no purpose, it's just there.
- $25,000 in an account with no purpose, it's just there.
- $50,000 in an account with no purpose, it's just there.
- $100,000 in an account with no purpose, it's just there.
- $500,000 in an account with no purpose, it's just there.

What showed up for you in this exercise? Many people discover a shift in what's possible when they reach a certain amount. It's different for each person, but more often than not, as the amount increases, folks shift away from a "That's a drop in the bucket" or "Wahoo, bonus!" mentality of saying they will spend the money to make a purchase, pay off debt, take a trip, or do a house project. Thinking about a larger amount of money often opens up more possibilities. When the amount gets high enough, people talk about having the best of all worlds. Now they're noticing thoughts like paying off debt, making a substantial purchase in cash, investing in retirement or future money goals, and being generous with others. At what amount did money open up more possibilities like this for you?

Completed solo or as part of a couple, this exercise can be eye-opening when it comes to priorities. For couples, it can highlight a partner's values and reveal what feels most important to them in life. In the stories we've shared in the book so far, we occasionally referenced values-based spending and saving. This is what we mean! When something is valuable and heartfelt for you, you are more willing to follow through, which makes you more successful at meeting your goals.

Is your value parenting? If so, investing in a house you can make into a home may feel important. Is your value family? In that case, taking care of your parents financially as they age is likely a top priority. Do you value freedom? If so, having a certain amount in savings may reinforce spending money or seeking travel as desired. Is your top value personal growth? Having an account for experiences like taking a class, learning a language, or continuing your education may feel worthwhile and fulfilling. The possibilities are truly endless, and this exercise takes into account the "why" of people's spending and saving priorities.

Ones: Are there other amounts you'd add to the list? Notice any guilt and respond with self-compassion.

Twos: At what number do you feel balanced in helping others and being financially stable yourself?

Threes: What number do you associate with success? What number do you associate with freedom? Why?

Fours: How would this money help you develop deeper connections in your life?

Fives: What amount makes you feel like you have enough?

Sixes: Your strength is in playing things through. How would each of these money milestones change your life and in what ways?

Sevens: At which number do you feel playful and financially free? Why?

Eights: How can you lean into vulnerability around spending, saving, and financial risks?

Nines: You think of others first. What would you do for yourself with one of these amounts of money?

Self-Preservation: Which number value made you feel secure? What do you think it would be like to actually save that amount? Is there any amount of money saved in which you would really feel secure?

Social: Which value made you feel you could really have influence and make important contributions? How would that change your life or the lives of others?

One-to-One: At what point did you feel even more likely to take big risks? What would it be like to either save the money or invest in a stable option? What about something that may be "high-risk, high-reward"?

Nguyen

Nguyen has a significant amount of money saved from his professional career so far. He knows from brief talks with friends that he is doing better financially than many people his age—he has saved over a year's worth of income, and he continues to receive investing advice from his uncle that has worked in his favor.

Even though his numbers look good, Nguyen is still struggling to feel comforted by each money milestone. He isn't sure what truly feels like "enough" until he engages in the Money Barometer exercise. From this exercise, he discovers that any number below what he's already saved doesn't feel emotionally significant. It isn't until he gets to higher figures that he recognizes a shift inside himself. When he gets there, Nguyen feels a loosening in his chest and takes a fuller breath due to finally feeling financially secure.

Make a Money Meeting

This final exercise isn't revolutionary, but it does pinpoint our learned behavior when we engage in meetings about money. Notice your reactions to the phrase make a money meeting. Did you cringe? Want to dig in your heels? Feel like cursing? Cross your arms? Forget to breathe? Stiffly say "No thank you"? These are common responses we see in our client work because of the ingrained association many people have between money and meetings and feelings like anxiety, shame, and dread.

Perhaps you thought of an accounting meeting or a meeting with a tax person? No offense to these professionals, but many people aren't eager to meet with them. People often associate these conversations with difficult conversations and shame, based on in their lived experience and memory. The meetings often feel mandatory, and our self-talk is something like "Let's just get through this, hopefully it will be over quickly."

The grit-your-teeth-and-get-through-it approach is something we want to eliminate with our Money Meeting exercise. We don't want these meetings to feel full of dread and anxiety; rather, we want to recondition our brains and nervous systems to regard money meetings as neutral—and hopefully attach pleasant feelings to them sometime in the future. Shifting to neutral from dread is a good first goal.

When you make a money meeting, what can you incorporate from your five senses to make it more pleasant? More tolerable? Manageable? What can you taste, smell, hear, see, and touch? Is it about having a certain snack? Being in your house, a coffee shop, your office, or in nature? Do you want music or silence? A candle burning? Fuzzy slippers and sweatpants?

Your first money meeting isn't meant to be a lengthy one either. Most folks start with a five-minute check-in with themselves on something related to money. Does this look like sitting and thinking about what amount to spend at the grocery store? Deciding what to do with a tax return? Checking your online bank accounts? Counting your cash in a savings envelope or piggy bank?

As you build more confidence and enjoyment into money meetings, you might have longer ones. Now you might be running a profit and loss statement for your business on a monthly basis. Reconciling your books as a small business owner. Reviewing a budget or spending plan with your spouse. Opening a savings account for a vacation you have planned.

In one of our most memorable client conversations about money meetings, the client talked about her idea of having a money date with their spouse, naked. We responded by asking her how she thought it would go. The client smiled and said she and her spouse would probably get distracted. We grinned and said her spouse might be more willing to have additional money meetings if they were scheduled this way.

All playfulness aside, are there incentives for before or after your money meeting that increase the likelihood of following through? Only one way to find out! Have fun with it! There isn't a wrong way to have a money meeting if it allows you to have the meeting and work toward the goals of said meeting. Ask yourself: What do you need for a productive and pleasant money meeting in the next week?

Ones: Can you think of a setting where you feel self-permission to be more spontaneous and playful?

Twos: Start with a solo meeting, even though you'd rather include a partner.

Threes: Approach this meeting as fluid rather than a one-and-done to-do list item.

Fours: What senses help you foster a greater sense of intimacy with a partner?

Fives: How can you embrace the vulnerability of asking for help? Does your meeting include a professional?

Sixes: Ask yourself, "What if this were easy?" Be aware of your tendency to depend on a partner or authority figure or, conversely, mistrust another's way of managing money.

Sevens: Have a few bullet points to keep things on track.

Eights: What's a shared financial goal you can craft together with a partner or family member? How can you rely on another person to help you achieve your goal?

Nines: Complete a values exercise (consider our exercise in Chapter 16) as your first money meeting. Now you have some anchors for what's most important to you.

Self-Preservation: Risk being vulnerable with someone about your finances. What does it feel like to ask for help?

Social: Resist the urge to consult with multiple people before your meeting. Come in with your own ideas before engaging a partner, family member, friend, or professional.

One-to-One: What boundaries might be helpful for this meeting? How can you regulate your emotions before, during, and after the meeting?

Scott

Scott has years of experience in construction and seasonal jobs. Because of his varying and unpredictable income, it is difficult for him to save or plan ahead for his future. His wife, Maddie, feels frustrated that they can't succeed at a budget together. Previous attempts at budgeting have led to conflict, with Scott retreating to his woodshop to be alone.

Scott listens to a podcast on his way to work that speaks of couples and finances. He learns that a shared financial goal improves couples' relationships significantly. He likes the podcast guest's playful suggestion of a low-risk money meeting in a setting that both members of a couple can enjoy. Scott knows Maddie likes a coffee shop just outside their neighborhood and suggests they try a quick budgeting meeting over their favorite drinks. Maddie is thrilled and shares that she's feeling optimistic that this time could be different.

Next Steps

All three of these exercises can be revisited again and again to see how things are shifting in your money work. We like to emphasize that money meetings are an ongoing, healthy practice for individuals and couples, so finding the right combination of pleasant sensory input and productivity is important. It's probable that money meetings focus on saving, spending, and earning more money. In the next three chapters, we will introduce additional strategies to improve your relationship with money—and leaving your former underearner identity behind you.

Chapter

Strategies for Saving

In a world built for instant gratification, it's hard for many of us to wait patiently for things to happen. On the other hand, planning for something down the road can feel rewarding—for instance, confirming the details of a vacation can sometimes feel more exciting than the trip itself! So how can we make saving more successful for folks who struggle to play the long game or who find it difficult to say to themselves, "It's worth the wait"? In this chapter, let's look at three strategies for successfully saving more money.

Renaming for Reframing

One part of the recipe for saving success is knowing what you are saving for. Are you saving for an "emergency fund" or "retirement"? Notice what emotions you attached to these words as you read them. Maybe there's an absence of emotion or worse, negative emotions associated with these words!

In this exercise, we invite you to rename your accounts with words or phrases that evoke a neutral or positive emotional response. Instead of "retirement," you might think about what your life would look like once retired, such as how you'd spend your free time, and spell that out as the nickname on the account. Instead of "emergency fund," which brings on anxiety and worry for many, what's a word or phrase that you find comforting? What's a word that would motivate you to save in this way?

Here are some word and phrase examples:

- Emergency fund: cushion, stability, comfort, peace of mind, rainy day fund
- Retirement: sailing, financial freedom, world cruise, unlimited travel, peace of mind, active grandparenting, flexibility, zero Fs, second life fund

What emotional responses did you have with these examples? What word or phrase best fits what you are saving for down the road? Try on a few phrases by writing them down and noticing any sensations in your body. If you bank with a large institution, you can nickname accounts any time you want, so try these on and notice how you feel when you log in and see them. If the phrase isn't working or doesn't have the same motivational energy you are looking for over time, switch it up.

After living through COVID-19, some folks struggle to think far ahead. Even looking just five years into the future can be challenging. If this is the case for you, saving for more immediate needs or smaller milestones can improve your saving success through emotional buy-in and increased confidence. This approach also serves as active practice for folks who have struggled to save money in the past.

So, what are you saving for in the short term? A new fridge? A car? A vacation? Concert tickets? Home improvements? A family reunion? A cooking class? Moving? Dental work? College? Time off? A destination wedding? Visiting family? Date nights? Try to think of a word or phrase that captures your savings goal.

Here are some examples we've heard from folks:

- Life-changing trip to Tuscany
- Family trip to Disneyland
- Turning our house into a home
- Dream kitchen
- Start a family fund
- Begin my new career
- Concert season
- Powder blue [make and model] car
- Future baby account
- Self-care account

Just like with the long-term savings strategy, seeing a word or phrase that reminds us of what we are working so hard to save for increases emotional buy-in and follow-through. Now's the time to find a phrase and try it on. Add it to your online accounts system, or write it on the envelope where this money will live.

Ones: Give yourself permission to change what you are saving for as you hit your goal.

Twos: Are you saving for yourself or others? Why not both? Give yourself permission to dream.

Threes: How are you going to slow down and celebrate when you hit your savings goal?

Fours: What ritual can deepen your feelings of satisfaction when you meet your savings goal?

Fives: Check in on your emotions through the savings process. Do you notice anything?

Sixes: Saving feels reassuring for you. Stretch out of your comfort zone with a shorter-term goal that involves savings followed by spending.

Sevens: What's the longest you've saved for something? How will you celebrate surpassing that time frame?

Eights: What's one way you can surrender to saving?

Nines: Check in often on your word or phrase for saving. Make sure it's yours and not someone else's.

Self-Preservation: When you think about saving, you may feel a sense of relief. How can you reframe saving as something you are working toward instead of a way to prepare for or fight against potential misfortune?

Social: Saving for yourself also allows you to engage with others. How can you connect your individual goals to the greater community you're a part of to find more motivation to save?

One-to-One: How can you make saving a competition with yourself? Try to gamify the process to see what you can accomplish.

Roda

Roda loves concerts. She focuses her spending on experiences that bring her closer to her interests of art and music, especially when they involve the social connection she craves as an extrovert. So, when

Roda learns she can name a savings account for something she wants, it feels almost effortless to designate her account for future concerts.

After writing out several phrases, she lands on "live music with friends" for her savings account name because it brings a smile to her face. Roda also recognizes that the phrase energizes her when she sees the amount increase each month. This exercise leaves Roda knowing she'll meet her savings goal well before the official season starts up this year.

Paid Time Off (PTO) Account

A true game changer for professionals who work for themselves is the Paid Time Off (PTO) savings account. Small business owners and entrepreneurs struggle to take time off because they don't earn an income for missed days of work. Add in the experience of spending a chunk of money for the vacation itself, and people often determine they have to keep working instead.

What if this doesn't have to be the case? Let's change the narrative that says vacations are expensive and are not worth the time off. With rising rates of professional burnout, we can all do better about giving ourselves emotional and financial permission to take a break.

Enter the PTO account! How would your work-life balance change if you had a PTO account that had money transferred into it every month? How would you feel if you could pay yourself to take time away?

PTO accounts are magical for:

- Planned and unplanned time away.
- Maternity/paternity leave.
- Unexpected illness.
- Mental health days.
- Family/kids illness or needs.
- Slumps or slowdowns in workflow.

For each scenario above, professionals can determine how much income would be necessary to make up the difference from a full week's income. Then, they can transfer those funds from the PTO account to their business checking. Ta-da! Have a kid out sick this week and are short $600 of income? Move the money from the PTO account. Need a mental health day? Transfer funds to make it so! Ready for the family vacation? Your business pays you to go!

These transactions truly feel life-changing for many professionals who've told themselves for years that they "can't afford" to take time off. By saving money in a PTO account for all such circumstances, business owners can improve their physical and mental health through financial flexibility while also taking care of business.

Ones: How much money do you need to see in your PTO account before you'll utilize it? Decide on a number. When it reaches your goal, act on it even if it feels indulgent or excessive.

Twos: How does this account bring you comfort as you balance supporting others and your business?

Threes: Spell out the purposes of this account as its nickname to help you follow through on using these funds when needed.

Fours: How can this account help you have a restorative mental health day?

Fives: How can this account help you invest in learning something new related to your interests?

Sixes: What amount in this account replaces anxiety with comfort for you?

Sevens: How will you engage in rest and restoration by using money in this account?

Eights: How can you work on your business during the slow times with these funds as a buffer?

Nines: How can you embrace spontaneity using funds in this account?

Self-Preservation: Try to find balance. You may be tempted to overindulge in self-care days, or you may be motivated to keep working so you don't miss an opportunity to make more money. Whichever side you fall on, what does it look like to intentionally lean the other way?

Social: How could creating this fund allow you to better connect with others? Be intentional about using it for yourself, even as you are motivated to be with other people or use it for them.

One-to-One: How would this fund serve your ability to maintain the energy and intensity with which you love to live your life? What boundaries might you need to put in place surrounding this fund?

Felicity

Felicity works for a local community college as a part-time counselor and has a small private practice on the side. Since she's started to feel burned out, she's considered moving into full-time private practice for the past several years, but she worries about financial stability.

In her work with her therapist, Felicity realizes she's operating from a scarcity mindset and hasn't calculated what she could earn on her own. When leaning into her numbers, Felicity stumbles upon a pattern of not taking time off because of the cost of her vacations. These considerations are adding to her burnout. She feels like she could turn a corner when she considers a PTO account that would allow her to take the time off that she needs, as well as pay herself for her absence from private practice to successfully reset.

Fill Your Buckets Funds

You've most likely heard of the Profit First model because of its popularity. In essence, it's moving money around in accounts several times a month and paying yourself first, before addressing monthly expenses. However, in our experience working with underearners, the framework it presents can feel intimidating and overwhelming for some folks. The number of calculations and transfers required every month to make it work can feel like a lot, especially to those who have previously lived in avoidance of their money. With this in mind, we'd like to introduce a simple, streamlined concept we call the Fill Your Buckets Funds.

Monthly Income—Monthly Expenses (including paying yourself!) = Fill Your Buckets Funds (FYBF).

Example: $6,000 monthly income—$4,500 expenses = $1,500 FYBF.

What would you like to do with the leftover money? Most folks want to keep some sitting in the business savings or checking account just in case. Some months there may be little to nothing left over due to lower revenue or periodic expenses; in this case, no further moving of money is required. But what about months where you have a remainder? What values-based priorities do you want to fund? Ideas:

- Short-term savings goals

- Long-term savings
- Pay off some debt
- Add to PTO account
- Spending bonus
- Self-care needs

Here are three reasons we love the Fill Your Buckets Fund:

1. **More than a Name**

Fill Your Buckets is more than a name, it's the practice of meeting multiple values or priorities at once. Oftentimes, you are filling your money buckets while also attending to your emotional needs. This can look like lowering your anxiety with a healthy savings account, giving yourself permission to take time off with your PTO account, or enjoying a bonus for all your hard work last month.

2. **Avoids Deprivation**

Unlike other savings strategies, FYBF isn't focused on reducing expenses first. Although we are fans of plugging leaks in your money flow (think forgotten subscriptions), ruthlessly cutting expenses leads to deprivation. Deprivation with money means to go without. To sacrifice. What do people typically sacrifice? Eating out and social contact that could be important for their mental health. Like a diet, this strategy tends to fail within thirty days, sometimes resulting in emotional spending in response to feeling confined and deprived of small-spend joys.

> **Small-spend joys** are items or experiences we spend money on that don't break the bank. It could be coffee, Legos, cards for others, skincare, farmers' markets, exotic chocolate, etc.

Additionally, we'd like to emphasize that in the FYBF model, you are paying yourself as part of your monthly expenses. Paying themselves is usually the first thing entrepreneurs and small business owners stop doing when money is tight. It's deprivation again, and it has a ripple effect on family life too. Although some people will embrace going lean to have more leftover funds at the end of the month, FYBF is more about being intentional with the funds that remain.

3. Supports Autonomy

With FYBF, there isn't a set amount or percentage that you must move to each of your buckets each month. This reduces the anxiety of not having enough to go around, and it gives folks the choice to fund the buckets that feel like a top priority each month. Perhaps one month you want to replenish your PTO account after being out sick for a week. The next month, you may want to put money into your long-term and short-term savings accounts. The month after that, you may decide not to move any money over based on the final amount. It's completely up to you every time, and just requires a simple money meeting on your part to decide.

Ones: What are the main priorities you'd like to fund? Why?

Twos: What funding buckets are for you and which ones focus on relationships with family and friends?

Threes: Embrace the small-spend joys. What brings you happiness amid the hustle?

Fours: How will spending from your buckets bring you deeper connection in your life?

Fives: What forms of spending have pleasant emotions attached? How can you embrace that more?

Sixes: How can small spending replace anxiety with excitement for you?

Sevens: You love fun! What is a practical bucket to fund to keep spending in balance?

Eights: How can you invite input from loved ones on how you allocate money to your funding buckets?

Nines: How can you prioritize one small-spend joy each month for yourself?

Self-Preservation: How can you allocate money to various accounts that are not restricted to savings or emergency funds? What other priorities do you have, and what would it be like to put money toward these areas of your life?

Social: Have an account that's for yourself as well as one for your business/family. You often think in terms of the group, so how can you balance prioritizing yourself as well as your community or organization?

One-to-One: Consider the long-term goals you have for yourself. How can you put more money away to enjoy at a later time instead of right now?

Trevor

Trevor moves to a new city to work for a small startup. He is highly motivated to contribute to the success of the product that he business is launching later this year. Although he's set to make more money with this company than in previous jobs, Trevor is determined to avoid his former burnout pattern of working too much and ignoring his social life. He is in a place financially where he can finally pursue hobbies and interests he's had for years, so he identifies one of his FYBF buckets for outdoor pursuits like sailing and playing golf with new colleagues and friends in his new home.

Chapter

Strategies for Spending

We hope the last chapter has inspired you with some strategies for saving! So many underearners struggle with both saving and spending, so we want to look at both sides of the coin within this book. This chapter is dedicated to helping you spend in ways that are aligned with your purpose, values, and goals. Before we present three strategies, let's slow things down with a money mindfulness exercise.

Emotional Awareness of Spending

How aware are you of any emotions that are present for you when spending? As humans, our emotions can influence our behaviors, including what we spend our money on. One financial therapist colleague shared that finances felt like 90 percent emotions, 10 percent logic—which rings true for so many of us. Mindfulness, often defined as the act of being present by slowing down, can be helpful as we get curious about our spending habits.

Questions to ask yourself, journal about, or reflect upon:
1. Recall your last purchase. What emotions show up when you think about it now?
2. When thinking of 1–2 purchases you made within the last month, what emotions do you recall feeling **prior** to shopping?
3. What emotions came up while spending?

4. What emotions showed up **after** spending?
5. What kind of spending brings up anxiety or guilt for you?
6. What are some things that bring you comfort or joy when you spend money on them?

Think of the comfort food many of us crave when stressed. In the same way, getting to know our emotional and situational drivers for spending can help us work toward changing our money story. By getting to know our spending habits through the lens of mindfulness, we come one step closer to embracing greater self-compassion about the emotions and behaviors money brings out in us on a daily basis.

Spending Plan for Shutting Down Shame

Speaking of emotions, what feelings come up for you when you hear the word budget? Is it another word that makes you cringe? Grit your teeth? Cross your arms in protest? If so, you're not alone! Budgets (at least how they are traditionally structured) support shame. You have a limit for groceries and exceed it, enter shame. You see that you have gone over on your coffee fund, shame. Eating out more this month than you planned? Here are red numbers all over your budget app and shame, shame, shame!

People are often surprised to hear that "budgets are bad" in the eyes of financial therapists. Setting limits reinforces a shame response—and these are oftentimes unrealistic limits that haven't changed in years to account for cost of living and inflation. "Why can't I do this? Why do I keep failing? I might as well not have a budget since I can't seem to stick to it." The shame of failing to follow through adds more avoidance of our money, which we already know is problematic.

So what is better than a budget? A spending plan! Financial therapists and other financial professionals aren't saying throw out your budget and wing it. Not at all. Instead, we recognize there's empowerment in knowing your numbers and having categories or line items for the things you need or want to spend money on.

Leaning into spending amounts reduces surprises. A spending plan can allow you to feel prepared and grounded instead of reactionary and ashamed when money is spent. How different would it feel to say, "Yep, I allotted $XXX for groceries this month and I got that right. I think I spend approximately $XX on coffee each month, I'm excited to enjoy it!" With a spending plan, we can successfully move from shame at exceeding a number we set for ourselves (a budget) to anticipation of having money for the things we find important, including small-spend joys.

What are some line items in your spending plan? Brainstorm or gather ideas from previous bank statements that reflect patterns in spending.

Ones: You can probably complete this exercise easily. What categories represent small-spend joys?

Twos: Do you have categories for connection and social time? What about self-care?

Threes: What line items would fall into a playful category for you?

Fours: What categories foster the deeper connection with others that you crave?

Fives: What line items have the most positive emotions attached?

Sixes: Having line items is calming for your anxiety. What categories allow for spontaneity?

Sevens: What name can you give the category meant for unexpected expenses?

Eights: What line items can be added by a partner, spouse, or family member?

Nines: Are small-spend joys represented in your spending plan? What are some examples?

Self-Preservation: How much of your spending plan is focused on comforts? What else do you need to prioritize?

Social: Your spending plan is only a small part of a larger system of your finances. Does it provide more freedom to view it this way? What changes might you make when you view spending in this way?

One-to-One: How does it feel to have a plan for the little things that bring you excitement in life? Practice being present to enhance your enjoyment of the things you spend money on.

Tatum

Tatum knows budgets don't work for her. When she tries to set one, she fixates on the numbers for a day, then ignoring them for the weeks after. At the end of each month, her bank likes to send some graphs of her spending to her inbox, which only makes her feel worse because she's ignored her budget completely.

Tatum is motivated to feel differently about money because she's tired of her inner critic calling her a failure. She watches a documentary on money that introduces an intentional spending plan, and something clicks for her. Instead of feeling shame for exceeding her budget, she feels more confident that she knows her numbers when she sees her spending match her estimations so closely each month. By embracing this strategy, Tatum can finally see what she spends each month and what she has left over. The new approach is helping her save for a trip with her sisters later this year.

Values-Based Spending

You've seen us reference values-based decisions on spending and saving throughout this book because they contribute to each person's internal and external motivators when it comes to money. Seeking clarity on what we want to spend our money on is important, whether it's small-spend joys or bigger savings goals.

Besides exploring how your Enneagram type informs some of your behaviors with money, completing a values exercise can add another layer of awareness of what feels important when spending.

Values Exercise Questions:
1. What values do you find most important in others?
2. Think of someone you respect or admire. Why do you feel that way?
3. Think of someone you don't like. What values do you think they hold?
4. What strengths do people say you possess? How do people describe you?
5. What feels most important in your personal life?
6. What feels most important in your professional life?
7. What values are you most proud to embody? Why?
8. If money wasn't a worry, what would you want to do for four hours a day?

Can you identify themes in your responses to the questions above? What stands out to you? Most people's values don't change dramatically in adulthood, so even if you've done a formal values exercise somewhere in your past, recall what values showed up then and compare them to your responses now.

Still unsure what values feel important? Take a look at the list of values below, noticing any emotional response or pull toward particular words. What do they have in common with your responses to the questions above?

Acceptance	Fairness	Perseverance
Achievement	Pleasure	Personal Growth
Advancement and	Power and	Play
Promotion	Authority	Privacy
Adventure	Fame	Prosperity
Affection	Forgiveness	Public Service
Appearance	Friendship	Purpose
Authority	Happiness	Rationality
Being in a Family	Having a Family	Recognition
Being Present	Health	Religion
Belonging	Helping Others	Respect
Challenge	Helping Society	Safety
Commitment	Honesty	Security
Communication	Independence	Self-Control
Community	Inner Harmony	Self-Acceptance
Competence	Integrity	Self-Respect
Competition	Intelligence	Service
Consensus	Intimacy	Simplicity
Cooperation	Involvement	Spiritual Growth
Courage	Knowledge	Stability
Creativity	Leadership	Taking Risks
Decisiveness	Location	Teamwork
Diplomacy	Loyalty	Time-Freedom
Education	Meaningful Work	Tolerance
Environment	Nature	Tradition
Ethical Practice	Neatness	Wealth
Excellence	Order	Wisdom
Excitement	Peace	

How does a values exercise contribute to your money story? In so many ways! If your top three values are personal growth, integrity, and education, for example, spending money on things that move these values forward will feel good to you. For this particular example, values-based spending could mean investing in a class, furthering your education, or pursuing a learning certificate in something of interest to you. Without forward momentum in your values, you could experience a loss of purpose and feelings of stuckness, and the impact on your mental health could be significant.

It's not enough to know what your top three to five values are. It's important to do a check-in on how present they are in your life at any given time. Living outside our values feels incongruent and exhausting for many, whereas embracing our values and keeping them as a top priority can feel enriching and fulfilling.

Once you've got a sense of your values, a clear next step involves asking how they are showing up in your spending habits. Does one value need your attention because it's currently absent in your life? Is there something that can shift to help you live more fully in your values? Do your values anchor your spending choices for here-and-now needs versus future plans? How can you adjust your spending to honor your values and what's most important to you?

Ones: What is a more balanced value for you than perfectionism?

Twos: Knowing your needs can be difficult. How can identifying your values lead you to a deeper understanding of yourself and what you need?

Threes: Where can connecting with your emotions show up in your values?

Fours: How are your values permission to pursue deeper connection?

Fives: What emotions come up when you examine your values? Why?

Sixes: How do your values encourage self-trust?

Sevens: What value(s) anchor you?

Eights: Can you think of a value that supports vulnerability for you?

Nines: How do your values contribute to your personal versus your professional self?

Self-Preservation: What values are you neglecting in your tendency to operate out of a need for safety and comfort?

Social: Which values represent you as a person versus you as part of a family, friend, or work group?

One-to-One: What values make you feel most connected to those you care most about?

Janise

Janise prides herself on demonstrating grit to meet her monthly commission in a fast-paced industry where competitiveness is high. She's worked for several companies over the years, and she feels the itch to reevaluate after being laid off unexpectedly during COVID-19.

She hires a career coach to help her explore her interests and completes a values inventory for added reflection. From this exercise, Janise realizes she has historically picked jobs that reinforce a behavior pattern of proving her worth, oftentimes resulting in fatigue and poor work-life balance. Janise acknowledges that her previous job didn't honor any of her values. This realization brings clarity to her latest job search, and she'd like to find something that feels like a better fit.

Pondering Periodic Expenses

Even when we are successfully saving and spending from our values, life can throw curveballs we don't always see coming. You've probably heard of forgotten or unexpected expenses being called periodic expenses. That's because these costs aren't always predictable and some happen "once in a while." Periodic expenses might come up once every six months or once a year, unlike the predictable monthly expenses. Other times, expenditures such as maintenance can become an immediate priority when something breaks. Let's look at some examples of periodic expenses that can skew a spending plan and add to your stress.

- Personal Life:
- Car maintenance
- Car registration
- New car tires
- Vet bill for your pet
- Annual memberships
- Insurance (life, health, car)
- Seasonal hobbies (ski pass, mountain biking, etc.)
- Summer camp
- Health and wellness (dentist, bloodwork, supplements, etc.)
- Donations (galas, seasonal events, scheduled times of giving)

- Weddings (destination weddings, being part of the wedding party)
- Tax filing services
- Small Business Life:
- Insurance
- Bulk order office supplies
- Printer/ink/toner
- Memberships and subscriptions
- Accounting fees
- Tax filing fees
- Small business annual registration
- Marketing
- Website hosting and domains
- Continued education/trainings
- License renewal fees

What would you add to the list based on your experience? One way to identify periodic expenses is to look at a full year of bank statements and make note of what came up within that year. Although this can feel daunting at first, this strategy can not only help you identify expenses with irregular timing, but it can also help you pinpoint when they typically show up in a year for planning purposes.

What comes next? For so many of us, periodic expenses feel reactionary. We don't always recall when they are coming due, or we don't plan for them and they reduce our account amounts or get charged on a credit card. This creates an understandable stress response. Below are three strategies for planning for these expenses. These approaches can contribute to a significant emotional shift from reactionary to preparatory when it comes to spending.

Strategy #1: Divide by 12

A common strategy for tackling periodic expenses is to estimate the overall cost of the expense and divide by twelve. This smaller number is the monthly amount that is then added as a line item to your budget or spending plan to represent the periodic expense in your monthly expenses.

An example would be an annual membership of $120. Divided by twelve months, this would be a $10-per-month expense. Some folks like to see this expense represented in their spending plan even though it's not being paid for each month. Others struggle with how these added line items make their monthly expenses look larger than they actually are in any given month. Recognize whether you lean toward or away from this option. If you're unsure whether it's for you, let's explore additional strategies for potential fit.

Strategy #2 Use Leftover Money

A second strategy involves taking your monthly income minus your monthly expenses and seeing what's left over to put toward unexpected or periodic expenses in any given month. When we discussed the Fill Your Bucket Funds (FYBF) strategy, we pointed out that the leftover amounts can vary. That's the biggest challenge here, and it makes it hard to plan more than a month or two ahead. Folks who embody Money Optimism may embrace this strategy the most, whereas others may want something a bit more predictable or planned out.

Strategy #3 Have a Periodic Savings Account

Our final strategy involves having a savings account (or envelope) for periodic expenses that you put money into every month.

Similar to the first strategy, there could be a line item stating how much you are putting in monthly (e.g., $25). However, in our financial therapy work, we've found that when a person gets to determine how much to put in each month, it works well from a place of autonomy and control. Some folks will do a monthly auto-pay amount, whereas others will move varying amounts each month to keep the account flush with funds for expenses as they arise.

The key here is to set a minimum amount each month to transfer or set aside, while encouraging ourselves to move more money over after an expense gets paid out of the account, or in anticipation of another larger amount being needed in the near future. This helps ensure the account has enough funds to serve its purpose.

Which strategy is most compatible for you and your life? Have you tried one and want to experiment with another? Does one sound more appealing to you based on your values and priorities?

Are you already using one of the strategies above? How is it working out? If it isn't working well, where can you try a new strategy within the next month?

As you can imagine, it's important to have some sense of your numbers before any of these ideas can stick. All three strategies support preparation over reaction when experiencing forgotten or unexpected expenses. In turn, these strategies support mental wellness because there is some money at the ready for when things come up.

Ones: Do you currently add the periodic expense category as a line item to your budget or spending plan? Is the amount working for you?

Twos: How do you define periodic expenses? Do you include money for helping others as part of this account? Why or why not?

Threes: You are likely to work more instead of accessing these funds regularly. How can this account support work-life balance for you?

Fours: How will you prioritize replenishing this account when needed?

Fives: What emotions does having a periodic expenses plan bring up for you?

Sixes: Notice what feelings come up as you move money around to pay for periodic expenses.

Sevens: How can you reinforce having a plan for periodic expenses with fun or joy for you?

Eights: How can a partner or family member inform the amount you put in your periodic expenses account or envelope?

Nines: How do these strategies help you prioritize yourself over others?

Self-Preservation: How might saving these funds help you be more calm when unexpected expenses arise?

Social: How do these funds serve your connection to your network? Do you consider funds connected to your community a periodic expense?

One-to-One: How might these strategies help you stay more organized with your money?

Shaye

Shaye is confident in her ability to budget and predict her monthly expenses. She sets regular money meetings and reviews her budget every quarter to prepare herself for the expenses that come next. She feels she's budgeting well until her car breaks down on the way to work one day. Shaye finds herself panicked and stressed when learning it will cost thousands of dollars to repair—thousands of dollars she has to put on a credit card to get by because she doesn't have enough in her accounts.

Shaye feels that having to pay interest on the credit card adds insult to injury, and she begins searching the internet for strategies that could reduce the possibility of this happening again with some other big expense. She comes across a video from a financial therapist who shares strategies for periodic expenses, and she feels seen when hearing that periodic expenses trip people up, even when they have a solid budget. Shaye takes in the strategies presented. She is excited to try them on for fit because they support her desire to feel in control with her money.

Chapter

Earn More Money

Up to this point, we've explored financial therapy strategies on how to save and spend money in ways that are aligned with your priorities. Now it's time to name the elephant in the room: What if you aren't making enough money to fund your lifestyle? What if you are putting in the work to save with intentionality and spend consciously, only to have your accounts in the red every month because you're not earning enough?

Often when working with underearners, we see a look of shock on their faces when they take a deep dive into their numbers and realize they aren't making enough money to break a debt pattern. It serves as a starting place for a shift in thinking when we uncover that their reliance on credit cards is justified because they don't have enough to pay their expenses each month. With this discovery, folks realize their inner critic has been attacking them about spending too much or not saving enough when, in reality, they aren't earning enough to break even!

Money Mindset Shift

When we find ourselves in a situation like the one described above, our inner critic demands that we cut expenses. But as we've already explored, that can lead to deprivation and result in self-sabotage when our efforts to cut costs are too extreme. People are wired to think,

"I'm $200 over budget, so I need to cut $200 in my expenses." Yes, this is a strategy and yes, this is also an example of deprivation. How do we shift to a mindset of "I'm $200 over budget, so I need to have (or make) $200 more this month."

Notice the changed emotional experience this new thought brings up. Do you find yourself moving from panic and anxiety to hope and determination? Does this scenario move from hopeless and out of control to motivating and in control? Do you hear an internal voice say "Challenge accepted" when thinking of ways to make $200 more this month? A mindset shift can have a positive ripple effect on how you relate to your money, especially when you consider the powerful interplay between thoughts, feelings, and behaviors.

Thoughts

Remember those money beliefs we explored in Chapter 1? Let's revisit them here as part of a mindset shift.

Examples of Money Beliefs:

- There's never enough money.
- Money doesn't grow on trees.
- I have to work hard for my money.
- Money is unpredictable.
- Money isn't stable.
- Money is bad.
- Money is corrupt.
- It's not about the money.
- We don't talk about money.
- Money changes people.
- Money is confusing.
- Money is controlling.
- Money is limiting.
- I'm bad with money.
- I can't hold on to money.
- I can't be trusted with money.
- Money should be saved.
- Money should be spent.
- Money is a tool.
- Money is transactional.
- I'm in control of my money.

- Money is necessary.
- Money is happiness.
- Money is power.
- Money is comfort.
- Money is stability.
- Money is freedom.
- Money is _____ (add your own).
- Money is _____ (add your own).
- Money is _____ (add your own).
- Money is _____ (add your own).

Which of these are positive? Negative? Neutral? Of the negative beliefs listed, circle the ones you've said to yourself. What belief(s) would you add? Is there one that's louder than the rest? How would you rewrite negative money beliefs to sound more neutral? What body sensations do you feel when you rewrite them and read them out loud?

Now, it's time to revisit the healing money scripts introduced in Chapter 4.

- Money Optimism: When it comes to money, It will all work out.
- Money Harmony: Money comes and money goes; money flows.
- Money Plentiful: There is enough money.

Which positive money script is most appealing to you and why? How would the core belief sound to you in your own thoughts and words? How would you know you are embodying this script rather than a negative money script?

Once you've identified the neutral and/or positive money beliefs and money scripts you want to adopt as your own, how can you reinforce them? Is it about saying the thoughts out loud? Writing them on a Post-it at your computer or on your bathroom mirror? Setting your word of the year or your intentions with them in mind? If we can reinforce the thoughts and beliefs that help us instead of hurt us, it makes it that much easier to address the driving feelings and resulting behaviors that come next when shifting our money mindset.

Feelings

One of the most triggering exercises in financial therapy is the net worth exercise. You may have heard of it or experienced it already, since some financial professionals ask clients to complete it when setting financial goals. If you are unfamiliar with this exercise, we will explain how it works in this section.

Why is the net worth exercise triggering? Because without a proper setup, it can reinforce feelings of embarrassment, anxiety, and shame. It can make people feel less than. It can encourage workaholism. It can reinforce the black-and-white thinking of "My net worth is my self-worth," which unleashes all sorts of problems tied to self-esteem, self-confidence, and mental health. People can get caught up in the numbers, asking, "What's my worth?"

Naming Net Worth

Where can the net worth exercise be helpful? Sometimes it's about leaning in or paying attention to feelings we'd otherwise prefer to ignore. In a way, this exercise serves as exposure therapy where the client experiences discomfort in smaller amounts for the sake of personal growth, such as building distress tolerance and increasing their insight. Although financial professionals would say this is a concrete exercise of numbers, financial therapists would counter by saying, "Yes, and."

Yes, it's helping people know their numbers and it's stirring up some emotions. Yes, it provides clarity and it's not a full picture of the client's money relationship. Yes, it's a strategy for measuring progress and it's one piece of a bigger money puzzle. Let's look at how the net worth exercise works:

Assets (what you own)—Liabilities (what you owe) = Net Worth

Assets are what you own:
- Your house's worth
- Your car's worth
- Money in checking
- Money in savings
- Retirement accounts
- Investments
- Life insurance policy
- Jewelry
- Family heirlooms
- Cash

Liabilities are what you owe:
- Mortgage
- Car loan
- Student loans
- Credit cards
- Personal loans
- Medical bills
- Other debts
- Money you owe individuals

Now it's your turn. Look at the formula again and use it to estimate your net worth. Assets (what you own)—Liabilities (what you owe) = Net Worth

In our work with underearners, we often see a negative net worth number to start. This is especially true when looking at homeownership and student loans if that's part of the person's experience. A negative number can, therefore, be normal. This exercise is most helpful when someone revisits it again as they tackle debt, save more, and/or earn more money. Seeing the numbers change in an encouraging direction can be very motivating and healing for a person who is used to negative feelings about their money story, including anxiety, avoidance, and shame.

Loud Budgeting

Another contributor to a mindset shift with money is loud budgeting, a phrase coined by Lukas Battle. The phenomenon, which started trending in early 2024, involves naming out loud when you can't afford something or, more accurately, when you have enough but don't want to spend money on the thing that's being asked of you.

Financial therapists, coaches, and mental health therapists know words have power, so we aren't here asking people to keep saying, "I can't afford this. I can't afford that." That self-talk has a negative effect on mental health and often keeps people living in scarcity. In contrast, loud budgeting is more about saying no and maintaining money boundaries for yourself and with others.

Consider how loud budgeting might work for you. What if it can serve as an empowerment tool? What if it helps you name out loud your values and priorities for saving and spending? Loud budgeting from this perspective could sound like:

- I don't want to prioritize that right now.
- I don't want to spend money on that.
- That's not a priority.
- I have other goals in mind right now.
- I'm saving my money for _____.
- I've already met my budget this month for (coffee/eating out/shopping/etc.).
- No thank you.

Owning your money goals and practicing boundaries with others sounds pretty exciting, doesn't it? Here's your invitation to experiment with loud budgeting from a place of owning where you stand. This tool isn't about reinforcing your ability to afford something; instead, it focuses on not wanting to purchase or prioritize something right now. It's a social response to financial peer pressure, and we love it. Loud budgeting and its mindset could contribute to a meaningful change in our feelings and behaviors about money.

Behaviors

With loud budgeting becoming a socially acceptable practice, we can get even more curious about how our behaviors with money can change. Does this practice give us self-permission to redefine wealth, as seen in Chapter 14? Can we anchor back into our values, as we explored in Chapter 16? Let's look at another strategy for knowing your numbers as it relates to behavior change.

Making Money Buckets

Not to be confused with the Fill Your Buckets Funds of Chapter 15, this money bucket exercise is much older and originates with financial professionals instead of entrepreneurs. You may have seen it in other places as the 50-30-20 model. However, we find those numbers problematic and triggering for folks whose percentages are higher based on cost of living, physical location, and inflation.

Instead of focusing on percentages, we help clients best support behavioral change by mapping out their current expenses. Now it's your turn. We invite you to draw three buckets (or purchase our Your Enneagram and Money Workbook) and think about what to name them.

- Bucket #1 covers everyday expenses and predictable monthly debts. Your bucket's name is _____(e.g. basic needs, current living, cost of living, everyday funds).
- Bucket #2 represents things that enhance your lifestyle and nourish your mind, body, and spirit. Your bucket's name is _____(e.g. self-care, nourish, next level living).
- Bucket #3 stands for your money future, including things like short- and long-term money goals, retirement, stability, and freedom. Your bucket's name is _____(e.g. future fund, financial freedom, wealthy).

Now it is possible to begin reflecting on your monthly expenses and deciding which bucket each expense lives in. Be sure to do an emotions and body check-in during this exercise to see if any feelings or thoughts are driving. Specifically, notice any feelings of shame, guilt, or worry, as well as thoughts of self-criticism and "shoulding" all over yourself.

Place each of your expenses into one of the three buckets and sit back to look at the full picture. Are all three buckets in use? Does Bucket #1 have the most expenses in it, which is what we would predict? Are there things represented in Buckets #2 and #3? Can you make any adjustments that would support your financial goals and work-life harmony? What surprises you?

After completing this exercise, one of our clients reflected that she saw nothing allocated in her Buckets #2 and #3. In other words, she could identify no items that nourished her (Bucket #2) or helped her move toward financial freedom (Bucket #3). This client was living in scarcity as she transitioned from being employed by someone else to working exclusively for herself as an entrepreneur. This discovery led us to some rich conversations about balance, her wants and desires for Buckets #2 and #3, and how small money goals could support her bigger vision of financial confidence and money flow over time.

Tasks or Time-Freedom

Speaking of entrepreneurs and small business owners, it probably doesn't surprise you that some underearners hold these identities—and the money behaviors that often go with them. We mentioned in Chapter 15 that business owners struggle to pay themselves when money is tight. It's often the first thing they stop doing when they need to make ends meet, and the result is that they may have a comforting amount of funds in their business accounts but a lack of money in their personal checking accounts.

As folks heal some of their money thoughts and feelings, they start to find their money flow with new behaviors. One of these behaviors is exploring the cost of their time over someone else's. When working to recover from professional burnout, I (Khara) remember a health coach telling me that people who are successful don't delegate tasks because they are lazy, but because they want to put their energy toward passions and pursuits that deeply matter to them. As a serial entrepreneur, this continues to resonate with me.

First, consider the cost for one hour of your time and weigh that against paying someone else. Is it worth the investment of paying another person for delegated tasks? Does it improve your mental health? Most often, our clients tell us that delegating supports time-freedom by allowing them to get some time back in their day. Having more time with friends, family, children, or pets. Engaging in hobbies. Finding more work-life harmony. If you are an underearner who is starting to make more money, the questions to ask yourself to embrace more time-freedom might sound like this:

1. What is the task that needs to get done?
2. How much time does the task require?
3. How enjoyable or unenjoyable is this task for me on a scale of 1 to 10 (1 very unenjoyable, 10 the most enjoyable)
4. What does it cost for me to do it? What would it cost for someone else to do it?
5. Do I want someone else to do it?

If your time costs $200/hour, for example, does it work in your favor to delegate a task you find unenjoyable that can be paid at $80 for the hour while you do something else? Does this look like prioritizing a client hour over an admin task, as one example? Hiring a house cleaner? Paying family for tasks around the house?

What thoughts or feelings come up for you with these possibilities? If you find that your inner critic is getting loud, practice self-compassion and get curious about why that's happening. It may mean revisiting the thoughts and feelings strategies shared earlier in this chapter a second time.

Are you ready to embrace the exercises above for a healthier money mindset? Completing each exercise can bring clarity to your money healing journey.

Ones: What's one way you can measure having a balanced money mindset?

Twos: How can earning more money help you and help others?

Threes: How will seeing your earnings grow continue to motivate new money goals?

Fours: How can you authentically ask for a raise at work or raise your rates in business?

Fives: What's one action step you can take to get closer to forward motion on earning more?

Sixes: You don't like to rock the boat. Looking to the future, what can earning more do for you and the people you care about?

Sevens: What priorities or money buckets will you fund when making more money?

Eights: Ask "What are your expectations" to a partner or family member when making plans for added earned income.

Nines: Based on your individual values, what's one thing you want to fund with your added income?

Self-Preservation: How would earning more money impact your anxiety? How can you shift your money mindset with your current net worth? Name what you already have.

Social: Who can you connect with to find more opportunities to earn more money? Set yourself a goal to reach out to at least one or two of your named people this month.

One-to-One: How can you channel your competitive side into creating new income streams? Can you connect with another person to engage in a true competition for making more money, or is this an opportunity to be self-competitive?

Chapter 10

Use Your Enneagram to Increase Your Earnings

How is your relationship with your money growing and changing now that you've completed the exercises in this book? We hope the tools provided here have you feeling hopeful and motivated to make changes as an evolving underearner who has so much money potential! Let's recap the concepts and financial therapy tools introduced throughout this book for you to revisit as often as you need to on your journey to a better relationship with your money:

Know Your Money Story
- Money Beliefs
- Negative Money Scripts
- Signs of Noble Poverty
- Signs of Scarcity
- Healing Money Scripts
- Warning Signs with Money (See Appendix B)
- Attachment Styles and Money
- Money as a Partner

Healing Financial Trauma
- Emotional Freedom Technique (EFT)
- Core Beliefs Exercise
- Dear Money Letter

Momentum with Money
- Money Word Association
- Money Barometer
- Make a Money Meeting

Strategies for Saving
- Renaming for Reframing
- Paid Time Off (PTO) Account
- Fill Your Buckets Funds (FYBF)

Strategies for Spending
- Emotional Awareness of Spending
- Spending Plan for Shutting Down Shame
- Values-Based Spending

Earn More Money
- Money Mindset Shifts: Your Future Relationship with Money
- Naming Net Worth
- Loud Budgeting
- Making Money Buckets
- Tasks or Time-Freedom

In addition to providing tools to help you heal your money story, we've shed some light on your money thoughts, feelings, and behaviors through the lens of the Enneagram. You took a deeper dive into the money beliefs, money scripts, and money behaviors of each Enneagram type and subtype to gain clarity on your current money patterns. You got curious about how your current (negative) money script could shift to a healthier script that serves you better, both financially and in life. You identified your values as they relate to your money choices of spending and saving. You dove into financial therapy tools for money healing. Finally, you learned how other underearners struggle with their money through the thought-provoking stories of individuals with Self-Preservation, Social, and One-to-One subtypes.

Money Maintenance
As you can imagine, your work around money is not a one-and-done experience. It involves regular money meetings with yourself and others, revisiting your numbers, and noticing your money beliefs as they pop up in response to financially stressful experiences. For example, what comes up for you when you think about the following?
- Holiday spending/gifts
- Car buying

- Homeownership
- Student loans
- Taxes
- Expensive airfare
- Attending a destination wedding
- Job loss
- Inheritance
- Welfare
- Medical emergency
- Family loss and grief
- Retirement

These are just some examples of situations where old money beliefs can creep back in unexpectedly, often in response to extreme stress. Since these situations aren't considered everyday money matters (for which you may have built a healthier narrative over time through exposure and repetition), they could stretch your healthiest beliefs about money to their limit, taxing you physically and emotionally. By noticing knee-jerk responses to these potential financial stressors, you're embracing another meaningful way to work on your evolving money story.

Money maintenance also requires talking about money, bringing shame into the light to lessen it, and leaning into the discomfort of learning new things when it comes to your finances. Here are two tools that can help you manage the emotional drivers of money:

Body Scan
When you find yourself steeped in negative beliefs about money, you may find it helpful to do a quick sensation check. Complete a body scan by bringing your awareness to your feet and moving slowly to the top of your head. Where do you feel that emotional response in your body? Where do these emotions live? What is each activation point trying to tell you?

Juliette
Juliette's sister is planning a destination wedding in Italy next year. As her maid of honor, Juliette is finding herself stressed about the expense of traveling internationally in addition to buying a dress,

attending a rehearsal dinner, securing lodging, and more. Juliette dreads the wedding planning calls with her sister, which surprises her because she was so happy to learn of her sister's engagement.

Juliette gets curious about her response before the next call by doing a quick body scan. She discovers a weight in her belly and tension in her jaw. The weight in her belly represents her dread and worry that the expense of traveling to Italy will set her back financially, and the tension in her jaw represents the unspoken concerns she needs to share with her sibling.

By sitting with the sensations, Juliette realizes she's trying to hold back and ignore her concerns about the cost of the wedding. Instead, she needs to name them in a thoughtful way so her sister can understand where she is coming from. This awareness results in a calmer internal experience for Juliette as she makes plans to communicate her worries to her sister hoping to find solutions they can both accept.

Shutting Down the Shame Monster

We all have a shame monster inside of us; it's also known as our inner critic. Often shame gets loud when we find ourselves without enough money, or when we make choices with money that aren't in alignment with our values. Shame is the precursor to avoidance of money because it feels bad. So here's another exercise that works well for shutting down shame, whether the emotion comes from money reasons or other emotional triggers!

1. Close your eyes or put them at rest.
2. Recall a recent time when you felt shame. What was happening? Where do you feel shame in your body? What mean things do you hear shame saying to you?
3. Visualize the shame monster behind the mean messages. What do they look like? Are they a person, place, or thing? What shape, texture, and color are they? Bring them into focus. What would you name them?
4. Now imagine a container to put them in. What color, size, and texture is the container?
5. Visualize placing your shame monster inside, then shutting the lid. Is it closed?
6. How do you feel now?

Tonya

Tonya is spiraling in her shame. She recently married her partner (they/them) of five years, and as a married couple, they've crafted a budget for their combined finances as well as their separate personal accounts. Tonya has a history of spending more money than she possesses, relying on credit cards to fill the gaps between paychecks. Her spouse, in their effort to help her, put together a detailed budget that accounted for all their expenses, as well as "fun money" for Tonya to use each month.

Tonya is midway through the month when she realizes she has run out of money. As she prepares to tell her spouse and explore the possibility of additional funds, she is flooded by shame. Tonya attempts to move her body in response to her discomfort. After a brisk walk, she decides to sit outside while speaking to her shame monster. Tonya closes her eyes and acknowledges her shame monster and the hateful things they are shouting in her ear. Then she states they aren't helping her and visualizes her container to place her monster inside. Through this unblending from her shame monster, Tonya feels more regulated and ready to speak to her spouse about her current money situation.

Shame doesn't have to drive our money decisions. Here are some additional tools and resources we've valued from colleagues that can become a part of your money healing toolkit:

- The Art of Money by Bari Tessler, Financial Therapist (book)
- Feel Good Finance: Untangle Your Relationship with Money for Better Mental, Emotional, and Financial Well-Being by Aja Evans, Financial Therapist (book)
- Financial Recovery by Karen McCall, Money Coach (book)
- Healthy Wealthy Talks Conversation Deck by the Pledgettes (thepledgettes.com)
- Let's Talk About Finances: Couples Edition Card Deck by Your Financial Therapist on Amazon
- Money Habitudes Quiz (moneyhabitudes.com)
- Money Attachment Quiz by Ed Coambs, Financial Therapist
- Money Healing Club with Rachel Duncan, Financial Therapist
- The Price of Avocado Toast podcast with Haley and Justin Brown-Woods

Although tools are helpful, the most important thing is to remain curious and compassionate so you can continue learning about yourself and your money story. This practice, in addition to the tools found in this book, will allow you to write your next financial chapter from a place of wellness, confidence, and increased self-trust.

Stay in Touch

We hope you are feeling seen in your struggles with money, with some ideas about where to go next. Your Enneagram edges can help you measure the warning signs to pay attention to, and they can also serve as a roadmap for customized, optimized money healing. Leaving your former underearner identity behind, you are bravely breaking the cycle of money beliefs and behaviors passed on to you from your family, friends, bosses, and society.

You are evolving into a healthier, more grounded version of yourself. We invite you to share your successes with us in our Facebook group *Your Enneagram and Money*. We know firsthand the magic of healing your current money story because we've lived it ourselves, and we can't wait to hear how it's helping you move closer to your own heart-led goals of financial stability and financial freedom!

·

Appendix
Enneagram Self-Discovery

Enneagram Motivations
1. To be good
2. To be loved
3. To be approved of
4. To be significant
5. To be competent
6. To be secure
7. To be happy
8. To be in control
9. To be peaceful

Thanks to the work of Beatrice Chestnut and Uranio Paes, we believe that there are twenty-seven different Enneagram types. This is because each of the nine Enneagram types can be broken down into three subtypes: Self-Preservation, Social, and One-to-One.

- **The Self-Preservation instinct** seeks comfort and security, is vigilant with safety concerns, and focuses on having control and structure in life.
- **The Social instinct** has a strong focus on community alliances and on one's position and relationship to the group.
- **The One-to-One instinct** is often referred to as the sexual instinct; however, we believe the term One-to-One depicts the core of the instinct well. Those with this subtype have a focus on close relationships.

You may have heard people describe their Enneagram **wings** as though this differentiates them from other people of the same type. Many people refer to wings as we refer to subtypes. We believe you have access to both wings (the two numbers directly adjacent to your primary type). If you have a stronger connection to one of your wings, it may be a good practice to begin to develop some access to your other wing in order to be more balanced and achieve growth.

The other important consideration when learning about the Enneagram is to understand the **passion of each type.** The passion is the emotional state that drives a person's thoughts, feelings, and behaviors.

The Enneagram can also be divided into different **Centers of Intelligence:**
- The Body Types (Types Eight, Nine, and One)
- The Heart Types (Types Two, Three, and Four)
- The Head Types (Types Five, Six, and Seven).

The Body Center of Intelligence is a group who uses gut intuition and energy to understand the world. Their primary focus is on justice and fairness.

The Heart Center of Intelligence primarily uses emotional intelligence, feelings, and relational connections to navigate the world around them. Their primary focus is on their image.

The Head Center of Intelligence uses logic, analysis, and thinking to interpret the world around them. Their primary focus is on security.

All About the Nine Types

This section provides more context for those who are interested in diving deeper into using the Enneagram for personal growth. Not all the terms mentioned here are discussed in the book; however, we are introducing them here for several reasons.

First, we know there is a lot of information out there about the Enneagram, and we want to help organize and simplify each type's information in one place. Second, we hope you will further your own study of the Enneagram by conducting research to learn more about the various terms. Finally, when trying to identify your type (which sometimes takes intentional work and diligent self-observation), viewing each type through the lens of these various categories and terms can sometimes be a helpful way to further narrow down your dominant type.

Type One

Type ones are motivated by a need to improve the world around them and be right (this is more about ethics than superiority). They are principled and industrious and often struggle with perfectionism due to their high ideals. All of us can struggle with limiting beliefs; however, Type Ones have a constant inner critic with standards that they try to live up to. They are in the Body Triad, which means their core emotion is anger. Since anger often is not appropriate, they try to ignore it, but it rears its head through their criticism of themselves or others.

- Basic motivation: To be right or good
- Basic fear: To be bad or wrong
- Orientation to time: Present
- Defense mechanism: Reaction formation
- Emotional passion: Anger
- Higher virtue: Serenity
- Harmonic group: Competency
- Harmony group: Idealist
- Stance (Hornevian group): Compliant/Dutiful
- Countertype: Sexual

Type Two

Type Twos are motivated by a need to be loved. They are warm and empathetic, often picking up on the emotions of others more than their own feelings. They are in the Heart Triad and interpret the world around them through emotional intelligence. Although they like to help others, they care more about maintaining connection and being valued than they do about simply helping.

- Basic motivation: To be loved/wanted
- Basic fear: To be rejected or unlovable
- Orientation to time: Present
- Defense mechanism: Repression
- Emotional passion: Pride
- Higher virtue: Humility
- Harmonic group: Positive outlook
- Harmony group: Relationist
- Stance (Hornevian group): Compliant/Dutiful
- Countertype: Self-Preservation

Type Three

Type Threes are motivated by a need to be worthy and look good in the eyes of others. They often try to accomplish this by being hardworking and earning their worth through success. They are in the Heart Triad but are uncomfortable with feelings because they slow them down. They can shape-shift to adapt to what their environment requires them to be. This can sometimes leave them with a sense of emptiness and a feeling that they don't know who they are.

- Basic motivation: To be successful and admired for their achievements
- Basic fear: To fail
- Orientation to time: Future
- Defense mechanism: Identification
- Emotional passion: Self-deceit
- Higher virtue: Veracity
- Harmonic group: Competency
- Harmony group: Pragmatic
- Stance (Hornevian group): Aggressive/Assertive—repressed feeling
- Countertype: Self-Preservation

Type Four

Type Fours are motivated by a need to be authentic and significant. They are intuitive, introspective, and resilient. They are in the Heart Triad and are comfortable with the whole range of human emotions. They are creative idealists, but this can sometimes leave them feeling that they are not enough, or that they somehow lack what others have.

- Basic motivation: To be significant and special
- Basic fear: To be ordinary or indistinguishable
- Orientation to time: Past
- Defense mechanism: Introjection
- Emotional passion: Envy
- Harmonic group: Reactive
- Higher virtue: Equanimity
- Harmony group: Idealist
- Stance (Hornevian group): Withdrawn
- Countertype: Self-Preservation

Type Five

Type Fives are motivated by the need to be competent and well resourced. They are consistent, logical, and discerning. They are in the Head Triad and are always thinking about and observing what's around them. They think that gathering enough knowledge will help keep them safe in the world, and they love to offer this knowledge to help others.

Fives need time alone to process and feel independent from others. Even if they don't get that time in a given day, they can retreat into their thoughts as an escape from the world around them. They begin each day with a certain amount of energy, so they try to conserve their resources so they are never without.

- Basic motivation: To be competent
- Basic fear: To run out of resources or not have what they need
- Orientation to time: Past
- Defense mechanism: Isolation
- Emotional passion: Avarice
- Harmonic group: Competency
- Higher virtue: Nonattachment
- Harmony group: Relationist
- Stance (Hornevian group): Withdrawn
- Countertype: Sexual

Type Six

Type Sixes are motivated by a need to be secure and have support. They are fiercely loyal, pragmatic, and strategic. They are in the Head Triad and use their thoughts to plan, so they are prepared for all possible outcomes. This type can struggle with anxiety more than some of the other types since they always anticipate things that can go wrong. Sixes tend to question people and the world around them. Although they can be perceived as pessimistic, they consider themselves realists.

- Basic motivation: To be safe and secure
- Basic fear: To be without support or unsafe
- Orientation to time: Present
- Defense mechanism: Projection
- Emotional passion: Fear/Anxiety
- Harmonic group: Reactive

- Higher virtue: Courage
- Harmony group: Pragmatic
- Stance (Hornevian group): Compliant/Dutiful
- Countertype: Sexual

Type Seven

Type Sevens are motivated by a need to stay positive and avoid suffering and pain. They are typically energetic and friendly, and their thoughts are usually steps ahead of everyone else. They are in the Head Triad and are always on the go; in this way, they avoid discomfort and are constantly entertained. They are independent and self-reliant, and because they are opportunists, they can sometimes struggle with commitment.

- Basic motivation: To be happy and have freedom
- Basic fear: To be trapped in pain or boredom
- Orientation to time: Future
- Defense mechanism: Rationalization
- Emotional passion: Gluttony
- Higher virtue: Sobriety
- Harmonic group: Positive outlook
- Harmony group: Idealist
- Stance (Hornevian group): Aggressive/Assertive
- Countertype: Social

Type Eight

Type Eights are motivated by a need to protect, control, and avoid being controlled. They are dynamic, natural leaders and are concerned with power—who has it and who doesn't. They feel deeply uncomfortable with vulnerability, so they often use their energy to protect themselves and others. They strongly care about justice and are not afraid of stepping into conflict to preserve fairness. They can sometimes be perceived as overly assertive because of their quick access to anger and intensity, but they are caring, protective, and will always fight for the underdog.

- Basic motivation: To be in control
- Basic fear: To be vulnerable
- Orientation to time: Future
- Defense mechanism: Denial

- Emotional passion: Lust
- Harmonic group: Reactive
- Higher virtue: Innocence
- Harmony group: Relationist
- Stance (Hornevian group): Aggressive/Assertive
- Countertype: Social

Type Nine

Type Nines are motivated by a need to be at peace both internally and externally. They are typically easygoing, warm, and practical. They do not tolerate conflict well and will withdraw when they feel there is friction happening in relationships or in the world. They value harmony to the extent that they suppress their anger even though they are in the Body Triad. They have a tendency to empathize with others so much so that they often lose their sense of self.

- Basic motivation: To have peace and harmony
- Basic fear: To be in conflict or disunity
- Orientation to time: Past
- Defense mechanism: Dissociation
- Emotional passion: Sloth
- Higher virtue: Right action (self-awareness)
- Harmonic group: Positive outlook
- Harmony group: Pragmatic
- Stance (Hornevian group): Withdrawn
- Countertype: Social

Appendix

Money Healing Journal Prompts

Consider the following journal prompts for money healing. Allow yourself to write freely, noticing thoughts, feelings, and sensations that come up.

1. How would you describe your current relationship with money?
2. What emotions do you associate with money?
3. What's one of your biggest money strengths?
4. What's one of your biggest money challenges?
5. What are your signs of scarcity?
6. What are your signs of noble poverty?
7. What's the best advice you've been given about money?
8. What's the worst advice you've been given about money?
9. What do you want for your future relationship with money?
10. What do you want to believe about money? Fill in the blank: "Money is _____."

Warning Signs with Money Exercise

1. What's it look like when I'm doing well with money?
   a. Physically
   b. Emotionally
   c. Relationally

2. What's it look like when I'm not doing well with money?
   a. Physically
   b. Emotionally
   c. Relationally
3. What are my triggers for backsliding into negative money scripts?
4. What can I do for myself when I'm struggling with my money behaviors?
5. What do I need from others?

ABOUT THE AUTHORS

Khara Croswaite Brindle, MA, LPC, ACS, CFT is a Licensed Professional Counselor and Approved Clinical Supervisor in Colorado. She is a Certified Financial Therapist through the Financial Therapy Association and enjoys various leadership roles within financial therapy to support the growth of the field, including financial therapy supervision, consultation, and her role as Director of Training for the Financial Therapy Clinical Institute. Khara has engaged her community as a mental health professional and clinical supervisor for the past 12 years in both community mental health and private practice settings. She is on a mission to support underearners including therapists in order to cultivate work-life harmony and a better relationship with money as business owners.

Hannah DeGroot is a Licensed Clinical Mental Health Counselor and Addictions Specialist in Colorado. After practicing therapy for several years and using the Enneagram as a personal growth tool for a decade, Hannah became a CP Enneagram Certified Coach. In addition to her therapy education, Hannah uses the Enneagram to Coach individuals desiring personal and professional development. Hannah is passionate about helping her clients find freedom from their anxiety, depression, addictions, burnout and negative self-image. In a short time with Hannah, you'll recognize her curiosity about people, animals, interesting foods and the outdoors. Before working as a counselor, Hannah was involved in human rights work in Uganda and has spent much of her life working with children and families in various capacities.

JOURNEY INSTITUTE PRESS

Journey Institute Press is a non-profit publishing house created by authors to flip the publishing model for new authors. Created with intention and purpose to provide the highest quality publishing resources available to authors whose stories might otherwise not be told.

JI Press focusses on women, BIPOC, and LGBTQ+ authors without regard to the genre of their work.

As a Publishing House, our goal is to create a supportive, nurturing, and encouraging environment that puts the author above the publisher in the publishing model.

Guide Point North Publishing is an Imprint of Journey Institute Press, a division of 50 in 52 Journey, Inc.

NOTE: The world of publishing has changed dramatically. This has also affected authors and their ability to let readers know about their books. Today, most people buy books based on word of mouth.

If you would like to help these authors, please consider leaving an honest review of this book on retail and book community sites.

www.ingramcontent.com/pod-product-compliance
Lightning Source LLC
Chambersburg PA
CBHW051204120626
46547CB00012B/1192